ROLAND BARTHES

ROLAND BARTHES
by
ROLAND BARTHES

Translated by Richard Howard

UNIVERSITY OF CALIFORNIA PRESS
Berkeley · Los Angeles

University of California Press
Berkeley and Los Angeles, California

Translation © *1977 by Farrar, Straus and Giroux, Inc.*
Originally Published in French as
Roland Barthes par Roland Barthes
© *1975 Éditions du Seuil*
All rights reserved
Published by arrangement with Hill and Wang, a division
of Farrar, Straus & Giroux, Inc.
Printed in the United States of America
First California printing, 1994

Library of Congress Cataloging-in-Publication Data
Barthes, Roland.
    [Roland Barthes. English]
    Roland Barthes / by Roland Barthes ; translated by Richard Howard.
        p.   cm.
    ISBN   978-0-520-08783-5
    1. Barthes, Roland.   2. Semiotics.   I. Title.
P85.B33A3   1994
410'.92—dc20
[B]   *94-7545*
                                                          CIP

08   07
10   9   8

The paper used in this publication is both acid-free and totally
chlorine-free (TCF). It meets the minimum requirements of
ANSI / NISO Z39.48-1992 (R 1997) (Permanence of Paper). ∞

My thanks to the friends who have kindly helped me in the
preparation of this book:
Jean-Louis Bouttes, Roland Havas, François Wahl, for the text;
Jacques Azanza, Yousseff Baccouche, Isabelle Bardet, Alain
Benchaya, Myriam de Ravignan, Denis Roche, for the pictures.

*Tout ceci doit être considéré
comme dit par un personnage
de roman.*

It must all be considered as if spoken by a character in a novel.

To begin with, some images: they are the author's treat to himself, for finishing his book. His pleasure is a matter of fascination (and thereby quite selfish). I have kept only the images which enthrall me, without my knowing why *(such ignorance is the very nature of fascination, and what I shall say about each image will never be anything but . . . imaginary).*

And, as it happens, only the images of my youth fascinate me. Not an unhappy youth, thanks to the affection which surrounded me, but an awkward one, because of its solitude and material constraint. So it is not a nostalgia for happy times which rivets me to these photographs but something more complicated.

When consideration (with the etymological sense of seeing the stars together as significant constellation) treats the image as a detached being, makes it the object *of an immediate pleasure, it no longer has anything to do with the reflection, however oneiric, of an identity; it torments and enthralls itself with a vision which is not morphological (I never look like myself) but organic. Embracing the entire parental field, such imagery acts as a medium and puts me in a relation with my body's* id; *it provokes in me a kind of obtuse dream, whose units are teeth, hair, a nose, skinniness, long legs in knee-length socks which don't belong to me, though to no one else: here I am henceforth in a state of disturbing familiarity: I see the fissure in the subject (the very thing about which he can say nothing). It follows that the childhood photograph is both highly indiscreet (it is my body* from underneath which *is presented) and quite discreet (the photograph is not of "me").*

So you will find here, mingled with the "family romance," only the figurations of the body's prehistory—of that body making its way toward the labor and the pleasure of writing. For such is the theoretical meaning of this limitation: to show that the time of the narrative (of the imagery) ends with the subject's youth: the only biography is of an unproductive life.

Once I produce, once I write, it is the Text itself which (fortunately) dispossesses me of my narrative continuity. The Text can recount nothing; it takes my body elsewhere, far from my imaginary person, toward a kind of memoryless speech which is already the speech of the People, of the non-subjective mass (or of the generalized subject), even if I am still separated from it by my way of writing.

The image-repertoire will therefore be closed at the onset of productive life (which for me was my departure from the sanatorium). Another repertoire will then be constituted: that of writing. And for that repertoire to be displayed (as is the intention of this book) without ever being hampered, validated, justified by the representation of an individual with a private life and a civil status, for that repertoire to be free of its own, never figurative signs, the text will follow without images, except for those of the hand that writes.

The demand for love

*Bayonne, Bayonne, the perfect city: riverain,
aerated with sonorous suburbs (Mouserolles, Marrac,
Lachepaillet, Beyris), yet immured, fictive: Proust,
Balzac, Plassans. Primordial image-hoard of childhood: the province-as-spectacle, History-as-odor, the
bourgeoisie-as-discourse*

*On such a path, a gradual descent toward the Po-
terne (odors) and the center of town. Here one encountered some lady of the Bayonnaise bourgeoisie walking
back up to her Villa des Arènes, a little package of Bon
Goût in her hand*

The three gardens

*"That house was something of an ecological won-
der: anything but large, set on one side of a considerable garden, it looked like a toy model (the faded gray
of its shutters merely reinforced this impression). With
the modesty of a chalet, yet there was one door after
another, and French windows, and outside staircases,
like a castle in a story. The garden, though continuous,
was arranged in three symbolically different spaces
(and to cross the boundary of each space was a significant action). You crossed the first garden to reach the
house; this was the "worldly" garden, down which,
taking tiny steps, pausing often, you accompanied the
ladies of Bayonne to the gate. The second garden, in
front of the house itself, consisted of narrow paths
curving around twin lawns; in it grew roses,
hydrangeas (that awkward flower of the southwest of
France), carpet grass, rhubarb, kitchen herbs in old
crates, a big magnolia whose white flowers bloomed on
a level with the upstairs bedrooms; here in this garden,
undaunted under their mosquito netting, the B. ladies,
each summer, settled into canvas chairs with their
elaborate knitting. At the far end, the third garden, except for a tiny orchard of peach trees and raspberry
bushes, was undefined, sometimes fallow, sometimes
planted with vegetables that needed no tending; you
didn't go there much, and only down the center path."*

The worldly, the domestic, the wild: is this not the
very tripartition of social desire? It is anything but
surprising that I turn from this Bayonnaise garden to the
fictive, utopian spaces of Jules Verne and Fourier.

(The house is gone now, swept away by the hous-
ing projects of Bayonne.)

*The big garden formed a kind of alien territory—
you might say that its chief function was to serve as the
burial ground for the extra litters of kittens. At the end,
a darker path and two hollow balls of boxwood: several
episodes of prepubescent sexuality occurred here*

What fascinates me here: the housemaid

*In old age, he grew bored.
Always coming early to table
(though the dinner hour was
constantly moved up), he lived
further and further ahead of
time, more and more bored. He
had no part in language*

*He liked writing out the programs for musicales,
or mending the choir music stands, boxes, anything
made of wood. He, too, had no part in language*

*One was good-looking, a Parisienne. The other
was good, a provincial: steeped in bourgeoisie—not in
nobility, from which she was nevertheless descended—
she had a lively sense of social narrative, which she
served up in a fastidious convent French, safeguarding
each imperfect subjunctive; gossip inflamed her with a
passion—an amorous passion whose principal object
was a certain Mme Leboeuf, the widow of a pharmacist
who had made a fortune in coal tar; this woman was a
kind of black flower bed, mustached and beringed, who
had to be lured to the monthly tea party (the rest in
Proust). In both sets of grandparents, language belonged to the women. Matriarchy? In China, long ago,
the entire community was buried around the grandmother.*

The father's sister: she was alone all her life

*The father, dead very early (in the war), was lodged in
no memorial or sacrificial discourse. By maternal intermediary his memory—never an oppressive one—
merely touched the surface of childhood with an almost
silent bounty*

The white snout of the streetcar of my childhood

Coming home in the evening, a frequent detour along the Adour, the Allées marines: *tall trees, abandoned boats, unspecified strollers, boredom's drift: here floated the sexuality of public gardens, of parks*

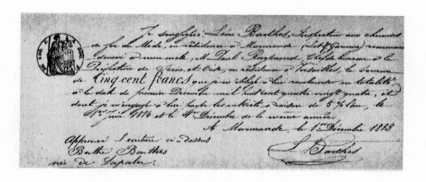

Has not writing been for centuries the acknowledgment of a debt, the guarantee of an exchange, the sign of a representation? But today writing gradually drifts toward the cession of bourgeois debts, toward perversion, the extremity of meaning, the text . . .

Where do they come from? From a family of no-taries in the Haute-Garonne. Thereby endowing me with a race, a class. As the (official) photograph proves. That young man with blue eyes and a pensive elbow will be my father's father. Final stasis of this lineage: my body. The line ends in a being pour rien.

*From generation to generation, tea: bourgeois sign and
specific charm*

The mirror stage:
"That's you"

From the past, it is my childhood which fascinates me most; these images alone, upon inspection, fail to make me regret the time which has vanished. For it is not the irreversible I discover in my childhood, it is the irreducible: everything which is still in me, by fits and starts; in the child, I read quite openly the dark underside of myself—boredom, vulnerability, disposition to despairs (in the plural, fortunately), inward excitement, cut off (unfortunately) from all expression.

I was beginning to walk, Proust was still alive, and finishing À la Recherche du Temps perdu.

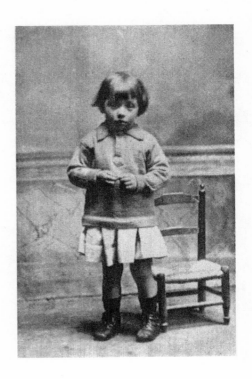

As a child, I was often and intensely bored. This evidently began very early, it has continued my whole life, in gusts (increasingly rare, it is true, thanks to work and to friends), and it has always been noticeable to others. A panic boredom, to the point of distress: like the kind I feel in panel discussions, lectures, parties among strangers, group amusements: wherever boredom can be seen. Might boredom be my form of hysteria?

Distress: lecturing

Boredom: a panel discussion

"The pleasure of those mornings in U.: the sun, the house, roses, silence, music, coffee, work, sexual quiescence, holiday from aggressions . . ."

Family without familialism

"Ourselves, always ourselves . . ."

. . . among friends

Sudden mutation of the body (after leaving the sanatorium): changing (or appearing to change) from slender to plump. Ever since, perpetual struggle with this body to return it to its essential slenderness (part of the intellectual's mythology: to become thin is the naïve act of the will-to-intelligence)

In those days, lycée students were little gentlemen

Samedi 13 Mai 1933.

*Darius, a part that always gave me terrible stage
fright, had two long declamations in which I was likely
to forget my lines: I was fascinated by the temptation of*
thinking about something else. *Through the tiny holes
in the mask, I could see only very high up, and very far
away; while I delivered the dead king's prophecies, my
eyes came to rest on inert—free—objects and books, a
window, a cornice, a piece of the sky: they, at least,
weren't afraid. I excoriated myself for getting caught in
this uncomfortable trap—while my voice continued its
smooth delivery, resisting the* expressions *I should have
given it.*

Where does this expression come from? Nature? Code?

Recurrent tuberculosis
(Every month, a new sheet was pasted on the bot-
tom of the old one; at the end, there were yards of
them: a farcical way of writing one's body within time.)

Painless, inconsistent disease, clean, odorless, id-
less; it had no other signs than its own interminable
time and the social taboo of contagion; for the rest, one
was sick or cured, abstractly, purely by the doctor's
decree; and while other diseases desocialize, tubercu-
losis projected you into a minor ethnographic society,
part tribe, part monastery, part phalanstery: rites, con-
straints, protections.

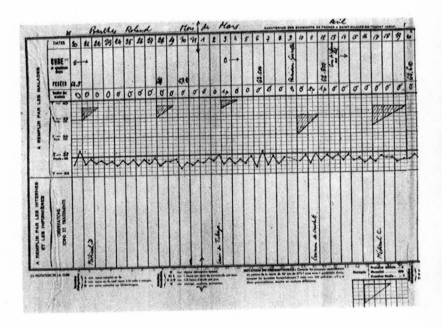

"But I never looked like that!" —*How do you know?*
What is the "you" you might or might not look like?
Where do you find it—by which morphological or ex-
pressive calibration? Where is your authentic body?
You are the only one who can never see yourself except
as an image; you never see your eyes unless they are
dulled by the gaze they rest upon the mirror or the lens
(I am interested in seeing my eyes only when they look
at you): even and especially for your own body, you are
condemned to the repertoire of its images.

1942

1970

My body is free of its image-repertoire only when it establishes its work space. This space is the same everywhere, patiently adapted to the pleasure of painting, writing, sorting

Toward writing

    According to the Greeks, trees are alphabets. Of all the tree letters, the palm is loveliest. And of writing, profuse and distinct as the burst of its fronds, it possesses the major effect: falling back.

> *A hemlock tree stands lonely*
> *Far north on a barren height.*
> *He drowses; ice and snowflakes*
> *Wrap him in sheets of white.*
>
> *He dreams about a palm tree*
> *That far in an eastern land*
> *Languishes lonely and silent*
> *Upon the parching sand.*
>
>   *Heine*

Left-handed

Actif / réactif ~ Active / reactive

In what he writes, there are two texts. Text I is reactive, moved by indignations, fears, unspoken rejoinders, minor paranoias, defenses, scenes. Text II is active, moved by pleasure. But as it is written, corrected, accommodated to the fiction of Style, Text I becomes active too, whereupon it loses its reactive skin, which subsists only in patches (mere parentheses).

L'adjectif ~ The adjective

He is troubled by any *image* of himself, suffers when he is named. He finds the perfection of a human relationship in this vacancy of the image: to abolish—in oneself, between oneself and others—*adjectives;* a relationship which adjectivizes is on the side of the image, on the side of domination, of death.

(In Morocco, they evidently had no image of me; my efforts, as a good European, to be *this* or *that* received no reply: neither *this* nor *that* was returned in the form of a fine adjective; it never occurred to them to *gloss* me, they unwittingly refused to feed and flatter my image-repertoire. Initially, this matte quality of human relationships had something exhausting about it, but gradually it came to seem a triumph of civilization or the truly dialectical form of erotic discourse.)

L'aise ~ Ease

Being a hedonist (since he regards himself as one), he seeks a state which is, really, comfort; but this comfort is more complicated than the household kind whose elements are determined by our society: it is a comfort he arranges for himself (the way my grandfather B., at the end of his life, had arranged a little platform inside his window, so as to obtain a better view of the garden while he was working). This personal comfort might be called: *ease*. Ease can be given a theoretical dignity ("We need not keep our distance with regard to formalism, merely our ease''), and also an ethical force: it is the deliberate loss of all heroism, *even in pleasure*.

Le démon de l'analogie ~ The demon of analogy

Saussure's *bête noire* was the *arbitrary* (nature of the sign). His is *analogy*. The "analogical" arts (cinema, photography), the "analogical" methods (academic criticism) are discredited. Why? Because analogy implies an effect of Nature: it constitutes the "natural" as a source of truth; and what adds to the curse of analogy is the fact that it is irrepressible: no sooner is a form seen than it *must* resemble something: humanity seems doomed to Analogy, i.e., in the long run, to Nature. Whence the effort of painters, of writers, to escape it. How? By two contrary excesses, or call them two *ironies* which flout Analogy, either by feigning a spectacularly *flat* respect (this is the Copy, which is rescued), or by *regularly*—according to the regulations—distorting the imitated object (this is Anamorphosis).

Aside from these transgressions, what stands in beneficent opposition to perfidious Analogy is simple structural correspondence: *Homology,* which reduces the recall of the first object to a proportional allusion (etymologically, i.e., in the Edenic state of language, *analogy* used to mean *proportion*).

(The bull sees red when his lure falls under his nose; the two reds coincide, that of rage and that of the cape: the bull is caught in analogy, i.e., in the imaginary. When I resist analogy, it is actually the imaginary I am resisting: which is to say: the coalescence of the sign, the similitude of signifier and signified, the homeomorphism of images, the Mirror, the captivating bait. All scientific explanations which resort to analogy—and they are legion—participate in the lure, they form the image-repertory of Science.)

Au tableau noir ~ On the blackboard

Monsieur B., teacher of the third form at the Lycée Louis-le-Grand, was a little old man, a socialist, a nationalist. At the beginning of the year, he solemnly listed on the blackboard the students' relatives who had "fallen on the field of honor"; uncles abounded, and cousins, but I was the only one who could claim a father; I was embarrassed by this—excessive—differentiation. Yet once the blackboard was erased, nothing was left of this proclaimed mourning—except, in real life, which proclaims nothing, which is always silent, the figure of a home socially adrift: no father to kill, no family to hate, no milieu to reject: great Oedipal frustration!

(This same Monsieur B., on Saturday afternoons, by way of amusement, would ask a student to suggest a subject for reflection, anything at all, and no matter how preposterous, he would always manage to turn it into a little dictation exercise, which he improvised as he strolled around the classroom, thereby testifying to his mastery of ethics and his ease in composition.)

Parodic affinity of the fragment and the dictation exercise: the latter will sometimes recur here, as an obligatory figure of social writing, a vestige of school composition.

L'argent ~ Money

Poverty made him a *desocialized* child, but not *déclassé:* he belonged to no milieu (he went to B., a bourgeois site, only for vacations: *on visits,* and as though to a performance); he took no part in the values of the bourgeoisie, which could not outrage him, since he saw them only as scenes of language, something novelistic; what he took part in was the bourgeois *art de vivre.* This art subsisted, incorruptible, amid every financial crisis; not misery, as a family experience, but embarrassment; i.e., a terror of certain terms, the problems of vacations, of shoes, schoolbooks, and even food. This *endurable* privation (as embarrassment always is) may account for a little philosophy of free compensation, of the overdetermination of pleasures, of *ease* (which is the exact antonym of embarrassment). His formative problem was doubtless money, not sex.

On the level of values, money has two contrary meanings (it is an enantioseme): it is very harshly condemned, especially in the theater (many attacks on the *théâtre d'argent,* around 1954), then rehabilitated, following Fourier, in reaction to the three moralisms which are set in opposition to it: Marxist, Christian, and Freudian. However, of course, what is defended is not money saved, hoarded, blocked; it is money spent, wasted, swept away by the very movement of loss, made brilliant by the luxury of a production; thus money metaphorically becomes gold: the Gold of the Signifier.

Le vaisseau Argo ~ The ship Argo

A frequent image: that of the ship *Argo* (luminous and white), each piece of which the Argonauts gradually replaced, so that they ended with an entirely new ship, without having to alter either its name or its form. This ship *Argo* is highly useful: it affords the allegory of an eminently structural object, created not by genius, inspiration, determination, evolution, but by two modest actions (which cannot be caught up in any mystique of creation): *substitution* (one part replaces another, as in a paradigm) and *nomination* (the name is in no way linked to the stability of the parts): by dint of combinations made within one and the same name, nothing is left of the *origin: Argo* is an object with no other cause than its name, with no other identity than its form.

Another *Argo:* I have two work spaces, one in Paris, the other in the country. Between them there is no common object, for nothing is ever carried back and forth. Yet these sites are identical. Why? Because the arrangement of tools (paper, pens, desks, clocks, calendars) is the same: it is the structure of the space which constitutes its identity. This private phenomenon would suffice to shed some light on structuralism: the system prevails over the very being of objects.

L'arrogance ~ Arrogance

He has no affection for proclamations of victory. Troubled by the humiliations of others, whenever a victory appears somewhere, he wants to go somewhere *else* (if he were God, he would keep reversing the victories—which, moreover, is what God does!). Transposed to the level of discourse, even a just victory becomes a bad value of language, an *arrogance:* the word, encountered in Bataille, who somewhere mentions the arrogance of science, has been extended to all triumphant discourse. Hence I suffer three arrogances: that of Science, that of the *Doxa,* that of the Militant.

The *Doxa* (a word which will often recur) is Public Opinion, the mind of the majority, petit bourgeois Consensus, the Voice of Nature, the Violence of Prejudice. We can call (using Leibnitz's word) a *doxology* any way of speaking adapted to appearance, to opinion, or to practice.

He sometimes used to regret having let himself be intimidated by languages. Then someone said to him: But without them, you wouldn't have been able to write! Arrogance circulates, like a strong wine among the guests of the text. The intertext does not comprehend only certain delicately chosen, secretly loved texts, texts that are free, discreet, generous, but also common, triumphant texts. You yourself can be the arrogant text of another text.

It is not very useful to say "dominant ideology," for the expression is a pleonasm: ideology is nothing but an idea insofar as that idea dominates. But I can go further subjectively and say: *arrogant ideology.*

Le geste de l'aruspice ~ The soothsayer's gesture

In *S/Z,* the lexia (the fragment of the text being read) is compared to that piece of sky cut out by the soothsayer's staff. This gesture appeals to him: it must have been a fine thing to see, in those days: that staff marking out the sky, the one thing that cannot be marked; then, too, any such gesture is mad: solemnly to trace a limit of which immediately *nothing* is left, except for the intellectual remanence of a cutting out, to devote oneself to the totally ritual and totally arbitrary preparation of a meaning.

47

L'assentiment, non le choix ~ Assent, not choice

"What is it about? The Korean war. A small group of French forces is on some sort of patrol in the North Korean highlands. One of them is wounded and found by a Korean girl, who leads him to her village, where the peasants take him in: the soldier chooses to remain among them, with them. *Chooses* is our language, at any rate. Not quite Vinaver's: as a matter of fact, we are in the presence of neither a choice nor a conversion nor a desertion, but rather of a gradual *assent:* the soldier acquiesces to the Korean world he discovers . . ." (Apropos of Michel Vinaver's *Aujourd'hui ou les Coréens, 1956.*)

Much later (1974), on the occasion of a trip to China, he tried to use this word *assent* again, to explain to the readers of *Le Monde*—in other words, of *his* world—that he was not "choosing" China (too much was missing for him to shed light on such a choice) but *acquiescing* in silence (which he called "insipidity"), like Vinaver's soldier, to what was under way in that country. This was not understood at all: what the intellectual public wants is a *choice:* one was to come out of China like a bull crashing out of the *toril* in the crowded arena: furious or triumphant.

Vérité et assertion ~ Truth and assertion

His (sometimes acute) discomfort—mounting some evenings, after writing the whole day, to a kind of fear—was generated by his sense of producing a double discourse, whose mode overreached its aim, somehow: for the aim of his discourse is not truth, and yet this discourse is assertive.

(This kind of embarrassment started, for him, very early; he strives to master it—for otherwise he would have to stop writing—by reminding himself that it is language which is assertive, not he. An absurd remedy, everyone would surely agree, to add to each sentence some little phrase of uncertainty, as if anything that came out of language could make language tremble.)

(By much the same sense, he imagines, each time he writes

something, that he will hurt one of his friends—never the same one: it changes.)

L'atopie ~ Atopia

Pigeonholed: I am pigeonholed, assigned to an (intellectual) site, to residence in a caste (if not in a class). Against which there is only one internal doctrine: that of *atopia* (of a drifting habitation). Atopia is superior to utopia (utopia is reactive, tactical, literary, it proceeds from meaning and governs it).

L'autonymie ~ Autonymy

The enigmatic copy, the interesting one, is the dislocated copy: at the same time it reproduces and reverses: it can reproduce only by reversing, it disturbs the infinite sequence of replicas. Tonight, the two waiters from the Café de Flore go to the Café Bonaparte for their apéritif; one has his "lady" with him, the other has forgotten to take his flu pills; they are served (Pernod and Cinzano) by the young waiter of the Café Bonaparte, who unlike them is on duty ("Sorry, I didn't know this was your lady"): everything circulates in familiarity and reflexivity, yet the roles remain inevitably separated. A thousand examples of this *reverberation,* which is always fascinating: barber getting a haircut, shoeshine boy (in Morocco) having his shoes shined, a cook making herself dinner, an actor going to the theater on the night his own play is off, a screen writer who sees films, a writer who read books; Mlle M., an elderly secretary, cannot write the word "erasure" without having to erase; M., a pimp, finds no one to procure (for his personal use) the subjects he furnishes his clients, etc. All of which is *autonymy:* that disturbing (comical and banal) strabismus of an operation that comes full circle: something like an anagram, an inverted overprinting, a breakdown of levels.

La baladeuse ~ The caboose

There used to be a white streetcar that ran between Bayonne

and Biarritz; in the summer, an open car was attached to it: the caboose. Everyone wanted to ride in that car: through a rather empty countryside, one enjoyed the view, the movement, the fresh air, all at the same time. Today neither the streetcar nor the caboose exists, and the trip from Biarritz is anything but a pleasure. This is not to apply a mythic embellishment to the past, or to express regrets for a lost youth by pretending to regret a streetcar. This is to say that the art of living has no history: it does not evolve: the pleasure which vanishes vanishes for good, there is no substitute for it. Other pleasures come, which replace nothing. *No progress in pleasures,* nothing but mutations.

Quand je jouais aux barres . . .
~ When I used to play prisoner's base . . .

When I used to play prisoner's base in the Luxembourg, what I liked best was not provoking the other team and boldly exposing myself to their right to take me prisoner; what I liked best was to free the prisoners—the effect of which was to put both teams back into circulation: the game started over again at zero.

In the great game of the powers of speech, we also play prisoner's base: one language has only temporary rights over another; all it takes is for a third language to appear from the ranks for the assailant to be forced to retreat: in the conflict of rhetorics, the victory never goes to any but the *third language.* The task of this language is to release the prisoners: to scatter the signifieds, the catechisms. As in prisoner's base, *language upon language,* to infinity, such is the law which governs the logosphere. Whence other images: that of choosing up hand over hand (the third hand returns, it is no longer the first one), that of scissors, paper, stone, that of the onion in its layers of skin without a core. That difference should not be paid for by any subjection: no last word.

Noms propres ~ Proper names

Part of his childhood was spent in a particular kind of listening: listening to the proper names of the old bourgeoisie of Bayonne, which he heard repeated all day long by his grandmother, infatuated by provincial worldliness. These names were very French, and in this very code nonetheless often original; they formed a garland of strange signifiers to my ears (the proof: I remember them very well: why?): Mmes Leboeuf, Barbet-Massin, Delay, Voulgres, Poques, Léon, Froisse, de Saint-Pastou, Pichoneau, Poymiro, Novion, Puchulu, Chantal, Lacape, Henriquet, Labrouche, de Lasbordes, Didon, de Ligneroles, Garance. How can one have an erotic relationship with proper names? No suspicion of metonymy: these ladies were not desirable, or even appealing. And yet, impossible to read a novel, or memoirs, without that special greediness (reading Mme de Genlis, I note with interest the names of the old nobility). It is not merely a linguistics of proper names which is needed but an erotics as well: names, like voices, like odors, would be the terms of a languor: desire and death: "the last sigh which remains of things," says an author of the last century.

De la bêtise . . . ~ About stupidity . . .

From a musical game heard each week on FM and which seems "stupid" to him, he realizes this: stupidity is a hard and indivisible kernel, a *primitive:* no way of decomposing it *scientifically* (if a scientific analysis of stupidity were possible, TV would entirely collapse). What is it? A spectacle, an aesthetic fiction, perhaps a hallucination? Perhaps we want to put ourselves into the picture? It's lovely, it takes your breath away, it's strange; and about stupidity, I am entitled to say no more than this: *that it fascinates me.* Fascination is the *correct* feeling stupidity must inspire me with (if we reach the point of speaking the name): it grips me (it is intractable, nothing prevails over it, it takes you in an endless hand-over-hand race).

L'amour d'une idée ~ Love of an idea

For a certain time, he went into raptures over binarism; binarism became for him a kind of erotic object. This idea seemed to him inexhaustible, he could never exploit it enough. That one might say everything *with only one difference* produced a kind of joy in him, a continuous astonishment.

Since intellectual things resemble erotic ones, in binarism what delighted him was a figure. Later on he would find this (identical) figure again, in the opposition of values. What (in him) would deflect semiology was from the first the pleasure principle: a semiology which has renounced binarism no longer concerns him at all.

Le jeune fille bourgeoise ~ The middle-class maiden

Surrounded by political upheaval, he plays the piano, paints watercolors: all the false occupations of a middle-class maiden in the nineteenth century. —I invert the problem: what is it which, in the practices of the middle-class maiden of those days, transcended her femininity and her class? What was the utopia of such activities? The middle-class maiden produced uselessly, stupidly, for herself, but *she produced:* it was her own form of expenditure.

L'amateur ~ The amateur

The Amateur (someone who engages in painting, music, sport, science, without the spirit of mastery or competition), the Amateur renews his pleasure (*amator:* one who loves and loves again); he is anything but a hero (of creation, of performance); he establishes himself *graciously* (for nothing) in the signifier: in the immediately definitive substance of music, of painting; his praxis, usually, involves no *rubato* (that theft of the object for the sake of the attribute); he is—he will be perhaps—the counter-bourgeois artist.

Reproche de Brecht à R.B. ~ Brecht's criticism of R.B.

R.B., it seems, always wants to *limit* politics. Doesn't he know what Brecht seems to have written especially for him?

"For instance I want to live with little politics. Which means that I do not want to be a political subject. But not that I want to be the object of a great deal of politics. Now one must be either the object or the subject of politics; there is no other choice; there is no question of being either both together or neither one; hence it seems indispensable that I should engage in politics and it is not even up to me to determine how much I should do so. This being so, it is quite possible that my whole life must be dedicated to politics, even be sacrificed to politics.''

His place (his *milieu*) is language: that is where he accepts or rejects, that is where his body *can* or *cannot*. To sacrifice his life-as-language to political discourse? He is quite willing to be a political *subject* but not a political *speaker* (the *speaker:* someone who delivers his discourse, recounts it, and at the same time notifies it, signs it). And it is because he fails to separate political reality from its general, *repeated* discourse that politics is barred to him. Yet out of this preclusion he can at least make the *political* meaning of what he writes: it is as if he were the historical witness of a contradiction: that of a *sensitive, avid, and silent* political subject (these adjectives must not be separated).

Political discourse is not the only kind to repeat itself, generalize itself, exhaust itself: as soon as there is a mutation of discourse somewhere, there follows a vulgate and its exhausting cortège of motionless phrases. If this common phenomenon seems to him particularly intolerable in the case of political discourse, it is because here repetition takes on the style of a *climax:* politics qualifying itself as the fundamental science of the real, we endow it, hallucinatorily, with a final power: that of checkmating language, reducing any utterance to its residue of reality. Then how tolerate with sanguinity the fact that politics too belongs to the category of languages, and turns to Prattle?

(For political discourse not to be caught up in repetition demands unusual conditions: either such discourse itself establishes a new mode of discursiveness: as is the case for Marx; or else, more modestly, by a simple *intelligence* of language—by the knowledge of its own effects—an author produces a political text at once strict and free, which assumes the mark of its aesthetic singularity, as if it were inventing and varying what has been said: this is what Brecht does in his writings on politics and society; or else, finally, that politics, at an obscure and even improbable depth, arms and transforms the very substance of language: this is the Text, that of Philippe Sollers's *Lois,* for example.)

Le chantage à la théorie ~ Theory blackmailed

Many (still unpublished) avant-garde texts are *uncertain:* how to judge, to classify them, how to predict their immediate or eventual future? Do they please? Do they bore? Their obvious quality is of an intentional order: they are concerned to serve theory. Yet this quality is a blackmail *as well* (theory blackmailed): love me, keep me, defend me, since I conform to the theory you call for; do I not do what Artaud, Cage, etc., have done? —But Artaud is not just "avant-garde"; he is a kind of writing *as well;* Cage has a certain charm *as well* . . . —But those are *precisely* the attributes which are not recognized by theory, which are sometimes even execrated by theory. At least make your taste and your ideas match, etc. *(The scene continues, endlessly.)*

Charlot ~ Chaplin

As a child, he was not so fond of Chaplin's films; it was later that, without losing sight of the muddled and solacing ideology of the character, he found a kind of delight in this art at once so popular (in both senses) and so intricate; it was a *composite* art, looping together several tastes, several languages. Such artists provoke a complete kind of joy, for they afford the image of a culture that is at once differential and collective: plural. This image then functions as the third term, the subversive term of the opposition in which we are imprisoned: mass culture *or* high culture.

Le plein du cinéma ~ Saturation of the cinema

Resistance to the cinema: the signifier itself is always, by nature, continuous here, whatever the rhetoric of frames and shots; without remission, a continuum of images; the film (our French word for it, *pellicule,* is highly appropriate: a skin without puncture or perforation) *follows,* like a garrulous ribbon: statutory impossibility of the fragment, of the haiku. Constraints of representation (analogous to the obligatory rubrics of language) make it necessary to receive everything: of a man walking in the snow, even before he signifies, everything is given to me; in writing, on the contrary, 1 am not obliged to see how the hero wears his nails—but if it wants to, the Text describes, and with what force, Hölderlin's filthy talons.

(No sooner have I written this than it strikes me as an avowal of the imaginary; I should have uttered it as a dreamy speech which seeks to know why I resist or I desire; unfortunately I am condemned to assertion: we lack in French [and perhaps in every language] a grammatical mode which would speak *lightly* [our conditional is much too heavy], not intellectual doubt, but the value which strives to convert itself into theory.)

Clausules ~ Clausules

Often, in *Mythologies,* the politics is in the last word (for instance: "So we see that the 'lovely images' of *Lost Continent* cannot be innocent: it cannot be innocent to *lose* the continent which has been rediscovered at Bandoeng"). A clausule like this must have a triple function: rhetorical (the scene ends decoratively), signaletic (thematic analyses are recuperated, *in extremis,* by a project of commitment), and economic (the effort is to replace political dissertation by a lighter ellipsis; unless this ellipsis is merely the casual method by which we leave off a demonstration *which is self-evident*).

In the *Michelet,* this author's ideology is dispatched in one (initial) page. R.B. keeps and evacuates political sociologism: he keeps it as signature, he evacuates it as boredom.

La coïncidence ~ Coincidence

I record myself playing the piano; initially, out of curiosity to *hear myself;* but very soon I no longer hear myself; what I hear is, however pretentious it may seem to say so, the *Dasein* of Bach and of Schumann, the pure materiality of their music; because it is my utterance, the predicate loses all pertinence; on the other hand, paradoxically, if I listen to Horowitz or Richter, a thousand adjectives come to mind: I hear *them* and not Bach or Schumann. —What is it that happens? When I listen to myself *having played*— after an initial moment of lucidity in which I perceive one by one the mistakes I have made—there occurs a kind of rare coincidence: the past of my playing coincides with the present of my listening, and in this coincidence, commentary is abolished: there remains nothing but the music (of course what remains is not at all the "truth" of the text, as if I had rediscovered the "true" Schumann or the "true" Bach).

When I pretend to write on what I have written in the past, there occurs in the same way a movement of abolition, not of truth. I do not strive to put my present expression in the service of my previous truth (in the classical system, such an effort would have been sanctified under the name of *authenticity*), I abandon the exhausting pursuit of an old piece of myself, I do not try to *restore* myself (as we say of a monument). I do not say: "I am going to describe myself" but: "I am writing a text, and I call it R.B." I shift from imitation (from description) and entrust myself to nomination. Do I not know that, *in the field of the subject, there is no referent?* The fact (whether biographical or textual) is abolished in the signifier, because it immediately *coincides* with it: *writing myself,* I merely repeat the extreme operation by which Balzac, in *Sarrasine,* has made castration and castrature "coincide": I myself am my own symbol, I am the story which happens to me: freewheeling in language, I have nothing to compare myself to; and in this movement, the pronoun of the imaginary, *"I,"* is *im-pertinent;* the symbolic becomes literally *immediate:* essential danger for the life of the subject: to write on oneself may seem a pretentious idea; but it is also a simple idea: simple as the idea of suicide.

One day, having nothing better to do, I consulted the *I Ching* about my undertaking. I drew the hexagram 29: K'an, The Perilous Chasm! (work at the mercy of magic: *of danger*).

Graphic bliss: before painting, music

Comparaison est raison ~ Comparison is motive

He makes an application that is at once strict and metaphoric, literal and vague, of linguistics to some remote object: Sadean erotics, for instance—which authorizes him to speak of a *Sadean grammar*. Similarly, he applies the linguistic system (*paradigm/syntagm*) to the stylistic system, and classifies the author's corrections according to the two axes of the paper; similarly again, he enjoys proposing a correspondence between Fourierist notions and medieval genres. He is not inventing, not even combining, he translates: for him, comparison is motive: he enjoys *deporting* the object, by a kind of imagination which is more homologic than metaphoric (we compare systems, not images); for instance, if he speaks of Michelet, he does with Michelet what he claims Michelet has done with historical substance: he functions by sliding over the entire surface, he caresses.

Sometimes he translates himself, doubles one phrase by another (for instance: *But what if I liked the demand? What if I had a certain maternal appetite?*) It is as if, striving to epitomize himself, he could not get it over with, heaped summary on top of summary, unable to decide which is the best.

Vérité et consistance ~ Truth and consistency

"The truth is in the consistency," Poe says in "Eureka." Hence if we find consistency insupportable we cut ourselves off from an ethics of truth; we abandon the word, the proposition, the idea, once they *set* and assume the solid state, *stereotyped* (in Greek, *stereos* means *solid*).

Contemporain de quoi? ~ Contemporary of what?

Marx: "Just as the ancient peoples experienced their prehistory in imagination, in *mythology,* we Germans have lived our posthistory in thought, in *philosophy*. We are *philosophical* contempo-

raries of the present, without being its *historical* contemporaries."
In the same way, I am only the imaginary contemporary of my own
present: contemporary of its languages, its utopias, its systems
(i.e., of its fictions), in short, of its mythology or of its philosophy
but not of its history, of which I inhabit only the shimmering reflection: the *phantasmagoria.*

Éloge ambigu du contrat ∼ Ambiguous praise of the contract

His first image of the *contract* (the pact) is more or less objective: sign, language, narrative, society function by contract, but
since this contract is generally masked, the critical operation consists in deciphering the confusion of reasons, alibis, appearances, in
short, the whole of the social *natural,* in order to make manifest the
controlled exchange on which the semantic process and collective
life are based. Yet, at another level, the contract is a bad object: a
bourgeois value which merely legalizes a kind of economic talion:
nothing for nothing, says the bourgeois contract: under the praise of
bookkeeping, of profit-making, we must therefore read the Base,
the Paltry. At the same time, and at yet another level, the contract
is ceaselessly desired, as the justice of a world finally "regular":
the preference for the contract in human relations, the security once
a contract can be interposed between them, the reluctance to receive without giving, etc. At this point—since the body intervenes
directly here, the model of the good contract is the contract of Pros-
titution. For this contract, declared immoral by all societies and by
all systems (except the most archaic), liberates in fact from what
might be called the *imaginary embarrassments* of the exchange:
what am I to count on in the other's desire, in *what I am for him?*
The contract eliminates this confusion: it is in fact the only position
which the subject can assume without falling into two inverse but
equally abhorred images: that of the "egoist" (who demands without caring that he has nothing to give) and that of the "saint" (who
gives but forbids himself ever to demand): thus the discourse of the
contract eludes two plenitudes; it permits observing the golden rule
of any *habitation,* discerned in the Shikidai passageway: *no will-to-
seize and yet no oblation.*

59

Le contretemps ~ The *contretemps*

His (admissible?) dream would be to transport into a socialist society certain *charms* (not *values*) of the bourgeois art of living (such a thing exists, indeed there once existed several): this is what he calls the *contretemps*. What rises up against this dream is the specter of Totality, which demands that the bourgeois phenomenon be condemned *entire,* and that any leak of the Signifier be punished.

(Might it not be possible to take one's pleasure in bourgeois [deformed] culture *as a kind of exoticism?*)

Mon corps n'existe . . . ~ My body exists . . .

My body exists for myself only in two general forms: migraine and sensuality. These states are not unheard of, but on the contrary quite temperate, accessible, or remediable, as if in either one it had been decided to reduce the glorious or accursed images of the body. Migraine is merely the very first degree of physical pain, and sensuality is for the most part considered only as a kind of reject-version of active pleasure.

In other words, my body is not a hero. The light, diffused character of pain or of pleasure (migraine too *caresses* some of my days) keeps the body from constituting itself as an alien, hallucinated site, seat of intense transgressions; migraine (as I am rather carelessly calling a simple headache) and sensual pleasure are merely coenesthesias, whose function is to individuate my own body, without its being able to glorify itself with any danger: my body is theatrical to itself only to a mild degree.

Le corps pluriel ~ The plural body

"Which body? We have several." I have a digestive body, I have a nauseated body, a third body which is migrainous, and so on: sensual, muscular (writer's cramp), humoral, and especially: *emotive:* which is moved, stirred, depressed, or exalted or intimidated, without anything of the sort being apparent. Further, I am captivated to the point of fascination by the socialized body, the mythological body, the artificial body (the body of Japanese costumes), and the prostituted body (of the actor). And beyond these public (literary, written) bodies, I have, I may say, two local bodies: a Parisian body (alert, tired) and a country body (rested, heavy).

La côtelette ~ The rib chop

Here is what I did with my body one day:

At Leysin, in 1945, in order to perform an extrapleural pneumothorax operation, a piece of one of my ribs was removed, and subsequently given back to me, quite formally, wrapped up in a piece of medical gauze (the physicians, who were Swiss, as it happened, thereby professed that *my body belongs to me,* in whatever dismembered state they restored it to me: I am the owner of my bones, in life as in death). For a long time I kept this fragment of myself in a drawer, a kind of body penis analogous to the end of a rib chop, not knowing quite what to do with it, not daring to get rid of it lest I do some harm to my person, though it was utterly useless to me shut up in a desk among such "precious" objects as old keys, a schoolboy report card, my grandmother B.'s mother-of-pearl dance program and pink taffeta card case. And then, one day, realizing that the function of any drawer is to ease, to acclimate the death of objects by causing them to pass through a sort of pious site, a dusty chapel where, in the guise of keeping them alive, we allow them a decent interval of dim agony, but not going so far as to dare cast this bit of myself into the common refuse bin of my building, I flung the rib chop and its gauze from my balcony, as if I were romantically scattering my own ashes, into the rue Servandoni, where some dog would come and sniff them out.

La courbe folle de l'imago ~ The imago's impossible graph

R.P., a Sorbonne professor, regarded me in his day as an impostor. T.D., today, regards me as a Sorbonne professor.

(It is not the diversity of opinions which amazes and excites; it is their exact contrariety; enough to make you exclaim, in the presence of such a reversal, *That does it!* and the pleasure such an experience affords is strictly *structural*—or tragic.)

Couples de mots-valeurs ∼ Pairs of value-words

Certain languages, it seems, possess enantiosemes, words which have the same form and contrary meanings. In the same way, for him, a word can be good or bad, without warning: the "bourgeoisie" is good when it is considered in its historical, ascensional, progressive role; it is bad when in power. Sometimes it happens that language itself provides the bifurcation of a double word: "structure," a positive value initially, has come to be discredited when it was apparent that too many people conceived it as a motionless form (a "blueprint," a "schema," a "model"); luckily "structuration" was there to take up the slack, implying the positive value par excellence: the *praxis,* the perverse expenditure ("for nothing").

Similarly, and more particularly, it is not the *erotic,* but *erotization* which is a positive value. Erotization is a production of the erotic: light, diffuse, mercurial; which circulates without coagulating; a multiple and mobile flirtation links the subject to what passes, pretends to cling, then lets go for something else (and then, sometimes, this variable landscape is severed, sliced through by a sudden immobility: love).

La double crudité ∼ Raw twice over

Crudity, in French, refers to language and to food; in reference to food it means *raw.* From this ("precious") amphibology he finds the means to hark back to his old problem: the problem of the *natural.*

In the field of language, denotation is really affected only by Sade's sexual language; elsewhere, it is merely a linguistic artifact; it then serves to render hallucinatory the pure, ideal, credible *natu-*

ralness of language, and corresponds, in the field of food, to the crudity (rawness) of vegetables and meats, a no less pure image of Nature. But this Adamic state of nourishment and of words is *untenable:* crudity is immediately taken as a sign of itself: crude language is a pornographic language (hysterically miming the pleasure of love), and *crudités* (as they appear on the menu) are merely mythological values of the civilized meal or aesthetic ornaments of the Japanese tray. Crudity therefore shifts to the abhorred category of the pseudo-natural: whence, great aversion for crudity of language and rare meat.

Décomposer / détruire ~ Decompose / destroy

Suppose that the intellectual's (or the writer's) historical function, today, is to maintain and to emphasize the *decomposition* of bourgeois consciousness. Then the image must retain all its precision; this means that we deliberately pretend to remain within this consciousness and that we will proceed to dismantle it, to weaken it, to break it down on the spot, as we would do with a lump of sugar by steeping it in water. Hence *decomposition* is here contrary to *destruction:* in order to *destroy* bourgeois consciousness we should have to absent ourselves from it, and such exteriority is possible only in a revolutionary situation: in China, today, class consciousness is in the process of destruction, not of decomposition; but elsewhere (here and now), to *destroy* would ultimately come to no more than reconstituting a site of speech whose one characteristic would be exteriority: exterior and motionless: in other words, dogmatic language. In order to destroy, in short, we must be able to *overleap*. But overleap where? into what language? Into which site of good conscience and bad faith? Whereas by decomposing, I agree to accompany such decomposition, to decompose myself as well, in the process: I scrape, catch, and drag.

La déesse H. ~ The goddess H.

The pleasure potential of a perversion (in this case, that of the two H.'s: homosexuality and hashish) is always underestimated.

Law, Science, the *Doxa* refuse to understand that perversion, quite simply, *makes happy;* or to be more specific, it produces a *more:* I am more sensitive, more perceptive, more loquacious, more amused, etc.—and in this *more* is where we find the difference (and consequently, the Text of life, life-as-text). Henceforth, it is a goddess, a figure that can be invoked, a means of intercession.

Les amis ∼ Friends

He is looking for a definition of the term "morality," which he has read in Nietzsche (the morality of the body among the ancient Greeks), and which he puts in opposition to morals; but he cannot conceptualize it; he can merely attribute to it a kind of training ground, a *topic.* This ground is from all accounts that of friendship, or rather (for this word is too stuffy, too prudish): of friends (speaking of them, I can never do anything but catch myself up— catch them up—in a contingency—a difference). In this space of *cultivated* affects, he finds the practice of this new subject whose theory is to be sought for today: the friends form a network among themselves and each must be apprehended there as *external / internal,* subjected by each conversation to the question of heterotopia: where am I among my desires? Where am I in relation to desire? The question is put to me by the development of a thousand vicissitudes of friendship. Hence is written, day by day, an ardent text, a magical text, which will never come to an end, a glittering image of the liberated Book.

Just as we decompose the odor of violets or the taste of tea, each apparently so particular, so inimitable, so *ineffable,* into several elements whose subtle combination produces the entire identity of the substance, so he realized that the identity of each friend, which made that friend *lovable,* was based upon a delicately proportioned and henceforth absolutely original combination of tiny characteristics organized in fugitive scenes, from day to day. Thus each friend deployed in his presence the brilliant staging of his originality.

Sometimes, in the old literature, we find this apparently stupid expression: *the religion of friendship* (loyalty, heroism, absence of sexuality). But since the only thing in religion which subsists is the fascination of the rite itself, he liked to abide by the minor rites of friendship: to celebrate with a friend the release from a task, the solving of a problem: the celebration improves upon the event, adds to it an unnecessary addition, a perverse pleasure. Thus, by magic, this fragment has been written last, after all the others, as a kind of dedication (September 3, 1974).

The effort must be made to speak of friendship as of a pure *topic:* this releases me from the field of affectivity—which could not be spoken *without embarrassment,* since it belongs to the order of the imaginary (or rather: I can tell from my embarrassment that the imaginary is very close at hand: I am getting warm).

La relation privilégiée ~ The privileged relationship

He did not seek out an exclusive relationship (possession, jealousy, scenes); nor did he seek out a generalized, communal relationship; what he wanted was, each time, a privileged relationship, marked by a perceptible difference, brought to the condition of a kind of absolutely singular affective inflection, like that of a voice with an incomparable timbre; and paradoxically, he saw no obstacle to multiplying this privileged relationship: nothing but privileges, in short; the sphere of friendship was thus populated by dual relations (whence a great wasting of time: he had to see his friends one at a time: resistance to the group, to the circle, to the crowd). What was wanted was a plural equality, without in-difference.

Transgression de la transgression ~ Transgression of transgression

Political liberation of sexuality: this is a double transgression, of politics by the sexual, and conversely. But this is nothing at all: let us now imagine reintroducing into the politico-sexual field thus

65

discovered, recognized, traversed, and liberated . . . *a touch of sentimentality:* would that not be the *ultimate* transgression? the transgression of transgression itself? For, after all, that would be *love:* which would return: *but in another place.*

Le second degré et les autres
~ The second degree and the others

I write: that is the first degree of language. Then, I write that *I write:* that is language to the second degree. (Already Pascal: "Runaway thought, I wanted to write it; instead, I write that it has run away.")

Today there is an enormous consumption of this second degree. A good part of our intellectual work consists in casting suspicion on any statement by revealing the disposition of its degrees; this disposition is infinite and in scientific terms we call this abyss opened by each word, this madness of language: *speech-act* (we open this abyss *first of all* for a tactical reason: to break down the infatuation of our statements, the arrogance of our science).

The second degree is also a way of life. All we need to do is change the focus of a remark, of a performance, of a body, in order to reverse altogether the enjoyment we might have taken in it, the meaning we might have given it. There is an erotic, an aesthetic of the second degree: (kitsch, for example). We can even become maniacs of the second degree: reject denotation, spontaneity, platitude, innocent repetition, tolerate only languages which testify, however frivolously, to a power of dislocation: parody, amphibology, surreptitious quotation. As soon as it *thinks itself,* language becomes corrosive. But on one condition: that it does not cease doing so *to infinity.* For if I abide by the second degree, I deserve the accusation of intellectualism (made by Buddhism against any simple reflexiveness); but if I take off the brake (of reason, of science, of morality), if I put the speech-act into *neutral,* then I open the way to an endless detachment, I abolish language's *good conscience.*

Every discourse is caught up in the interplay of degrees. We might call this interplay *bathmology*. A neologism is not superfluous if it gives us the notion of a new science: that of the degrees of language. This science will be unheard of, for it will overturn the habitual instances of expression, of reading, and of listening ("truth," "reality," "sincerity"); its principle will be a shock: it will straddle, as between one step and another, all *expression*.

La dénotation comme vérité du langage
~ Denotation as the truth of language

In the Falaise pharmacy, Bouvard and Pécuchet subject the jujube lozenge to the water test: "It assumed the transparence of a bacon rind, which denoted the presence of gelatin."

Denotation would here be a scientific myth: that of a "true" state of language, as if every sentence had inside it an *etymon* (origin and truth). *Denotation/connotation:* this double concept therefore applies only within the field of truth. Each time I need to test a message (to demystify it), I subject it to some external instance, I educe it to a kind of uncouth rind, which forms its true substratum. The opposition therefore functions only in the context of a critical operation analogous to an experiment in chemical analysis: each time I believe in the truth, I have need of denotation.

Sa voix ~ His voice

(No one's in particular. Yes, in particular! It is always someone's voice.)

I try, little by little, to *render* his voice. I make an adjectival approach: agile, fragile, youthful, somewhat broken? No, not quite; rather: *overcultivated,* having a faint British flavor. And how about this: clipped? Yes, if I expatiate: he revealed in this clipped quality not the torsion (the grimace) of a body controlling and thereby affirming itself but on the contrary the exhausting collapse of the subject without language, presenting the threat of aphasia under which he struggles: contrary to the first, this was a voice *without rhetoric* (though not without tenderness). For all these voices, the right metaphor would have to be invented, the one which, once encountered, would possess you forever; but I fail to find any such thing, so great is the gap between the words which come to me from the culture and this strange being (can it be no more than a matter of sounds?) which I fleetingly recall at my ear.

Such impotence has a reason: the voice is always *already* dead, and it is by a kind of desperate denial that we call it: living; this irremediable loss we give the name of *inflection:* inflection is the voice insofar as it is always past, silenced.

Whereby we may understand what *description* is: it strives to render what is strictly mortal in the object by feigning (illusion by reversal) to suppose it, to desire it *living:* "as if alive" means "apparently dead." The adjective is the instrument of this illusion; whatever it says, by its descriptive quality alone, the adjective is funereal.

Détacher ～ To detach

To detach is the essential gesture of classical art. The painter "detaches" a feature, a shadow, if need be enlarges it, reverses it, and makes it into a work; and even though the work is consistent, insignificant, or natural (one of Duchamp's objects, a monochrome surface), since it always extends, whether one likes it or not, beyond a physical context (a wall, a street), it is fatally hallowed as a work. In this, art is the contrary of the sociological, philological, political sciences, which keep *integrating* what they have distinguished (they distinguish it only to integrate it the more completely). Art is thus never paranoiac, but always perverse, fetishistic.

Dialectiques ～ Dialectics

Everything seems to suggest that his discourse proceeds according to a two-term dialectic: popular opinion and its contrary, *Doxa* and its paradox, the stereotype and the novation, fatigue and freshness, relish and disgust: *I like/I don't like*. This binary dialectic is the dialectic of meaning itself (*marked/not marked*) and of the Freudian game the child plays (*Fort/Da*): the dialectic of value.

Yet is this quite true? In him, another dialectic appears, trying to find expression: the contradiction of the terms yields in his eyes by the discovery of a third term, which is not a synthesis but a *translation:* everything comes back, but it comes back as Fiction, i.e., at another turn of the spiral.

Pluriel, différence, conflit ~ Plural, difference, conflict

He often resorts to a kind of philosophy vaguely labeled *pluralism.*

Who knows if this insistence on the plural is not a way of denying sexual duality? The opposition of the sexes must not be a law of Nature; therefore, the confrontations and paradigms must be dissolved, both the meanings and the sexes be pluralized: meaning will tend toward its multiplication, its dispersion (in the theory of the Text), and sex will be taken into no typology (there will be, for example, only *homosexualities,* whose plural will baffle any constituted, centered discourse, to the point where it seems to him virtually pointless to talk about it).

Similarly, *difference,* that much-vaunted and insistent word, prevails because it dispenses with or triumphs over conflict. Conflict is sexual, semantic; difference is plural, sensual, and textual; meaning and sex are principles of construction, of constitution; difference is the very movement of dispersion, of friability, a shimmer; what matters is not the discovery, in a reading of the world and of the self, of certain oppositions but of encroachments, overflows, leaks, skids, shifts, slips . . .

According to Freud (in the book about Moses), one touch of difference leads to racism. But a great deal of difference leads away from it, irremediably. To equalize, democratize, homogenize—all such efforts will never manage to expel "the tiniest difference," seed of racial intolerance. For that one must pluralize, refine, continuously.

Le goût de la division ~ Propensity for division

Propensity for division: fragments, miniatures, partitions, glittering details (according to Baudelaire, the effect of hashish), a bird's-eye view of fields, windows, haiku, line drawing, script, photography, in plays the "scene" *à l'italienne,* in short, depending on your point of view, all the articulation of the semanticist or all the raw material of the fetishist. This propensity is labeled *progressive:* art of the rising classes proceeds by just such framing (Brecht, Diderot, Eisenstein).

Au piano, le doigté . . . ~ At the piano, fingering . . .

At the piano, "fingering" has nothing to do with an assigned value of elegance and delicacy (which we refer to as "touch") but merely designates a way of numbering the fingers which must play this or that note; fingering establishes in a deliberate manner what will become an automatism: in short, it is the programming of a machine, an animal inscription. Now, if I play badly—aside from the lack of velocity, which is a purely muscular problem—it is because I fail to abide by the written fingering: I improvise, each time I play, the position of my fingers, and therefore I can never play anything without making mistakes. The reason for this is obviously that I want an immediate pleasure and reject the tedium of training, for training hampers pleasure—for the sake of a greater ulterior pleasure, as they say (we tell the pianist what the gods said to Orpheus: Don't turn back *prematurely* on the effects of your action). So that the piece, in the perfection attributed to it but never really attained, functions as a bit of hallucination: I gladly give myself up to the watchword of a fantasy: *"Immediately!"* even at the cost of a considerable loss of reality.

Le mauvais objet ~ The wrong object

Doxa (public opinion), much invoked in his discourse, is merely a *"wrong object":* never defined by its content, only by its form, and that invariably wrong form is doubtless: repetition.

—But what is repeated is sometimes good, for instance, the *theme* (a good critical object, the "right" object) is something that is repeated, isn't it? —The repetition that comes from the body is good, is right. *Doxa* is the wrong object because it is a dead repetition, because it comes from *no one's* body—except perhaps, indeed, from the body of the Dead.

Doxa / paradoxa ~ *Doxa* / paradoxa

Reactive formations: a *Doxa* (a popular opinion) is posited, intolerable; to free myself of it, I postulate a paradox; then this paradox turns bad, becomes a new concretion, itself becomes a new *Doxa,* and I must seek further for a new paradox.

Let us follow this trajectory once again. At the work's source, the opacity of social relations, a false Nature; the first impulse, the first shock, then, is to demystify (*Mythologies*); then when the demystification is immobilized in repetition, it must be displaced: semiological *science* (then postulated) tries to stir, to vivify, to arm the mythological gesture, the pose, by endowing it with a method; this science is encumbered in its turn with a whole repertoire of images: the goal of a semiological science is replaced by the (often very grim) science of the semiologists; hence, one must sever oneself from that, must introduce into this rational image-repertoire the texture of desire, the claims of the body: this, then, is the Text, the theory of the Text. But again the Text risks paralysis: it repeats itself, counterfeits itself in lusterless texts, testimonies to a demand for readers, not for a desire to please: the Text tends to degenerate into prattle (*Babil*). Where to go next? That is where I am now.

La Papillonne ~ *"La Papillonne"*

Crazy, the power of distraction a man has who is bored, intimidated, or embarrassed by his work: working in the country (at what? at rereading myself, alas!), here is the list of distractions I incur every five minutes: spray a mosquito, cut my nails, eat a plum, take a piss, check the faucet to see if the water is still muddy (there was a breakdown in the plumbing today), go to the drugstore, walk down to the garden to see how many nectarines have ripened on the tree, look at the radio-program listings, rig up a stand to hold my papers, etc.: *I am cruising.*

(Cruising relates to that passion which Fourier called the Variant, the Alternant, the Butterfly—in the feminine: *"La Papillonne."*

Amphibologies ~ Amphibologies

The word "intelligence" can designate a faculty of intellection or a complicity (*to have intelligence that* . . .); in general, the context forces us to choose one of the two meanings and to forget the other. Each time he encounters one of these double words, R.B., on the contrary, insists on keeping both meanings, as if one were winking at the other and as if the word's meaning were in that wink, so that *one and the same word*, in *one and the same sentence*, means *at one and the same time* two different things, and so that one delights, semantically, in the one by the other. This is why such words are often said to be "preciously ambiguous": not in their lexical essence (for any word in the lexicon has several meanings), but because, by a kind of *luck*, a kind of favor not of language but of discourse, I can *actualize* their amphibology, can say "intelligence" and appear to be referring chiefly to the intellective meaning, but letting the meaning of "complicity" be *understood.*

In French these amphibologies are extremely (abnormally) numerous: *Absence* (lack of the person and distraction of the mind), *Alibi* (a different place and a police justification), *Aliénation* ("a good word, at once social and mental"), *Alimenter* (to fill the pond and to nourish the conversation), *Brûlé* (burned and unmasked), *Cause* (what provokes and what one embraces), *Citer* (to call and to copy), *Comprendre* (to contain and to grasp intellectually), *Contenance* (possibility of being filled and way of behaving), *Crudité* (alimentary and sexual), *Développer* (the rhetorical meaning and the athletic meaning), *Discret* (discontinuous and restrained), *Exemple* (of grammar and of debauchery), *Exprimer* (to squeeze out a juice and to manifest one's inwardness), *Fiché* (nailed and filed with the police), *Fin* (limit and goal), *Fonction* (relation and use), *Fraîcheur* (temperature and novelty), *Frappe* (stamp and scamp), *Indifférence* (absence of passion and of difference), *Jeu* (ludic activity and the movement of parts in a machine), *Partir* (to leave and to be drugged), *Pollution* (stain and masturbation), *Posséder* (to have and to dominate), *Propriété* (property and propriety), *Questionner* (to interrogate and to torture), *Scène* (in a play and in a household), *Sens* (direction and signification), *Sujet* (subject of the action and object of the discourse), *Subtiliser* (to make more subtle and to purloin), *Trait* (graphic and linguistic feature), *Voix* (bodily organ and grammatical diathesis), etc.

In the dossier of this double response: the *addâd*, those Arab words each of which has two absolutely contrary meanings; Greek tragedy, the space of a double understanding, in which "the spectator always understands more than what each character utters on his own account or on that of his partners"; Flaubert's auditory manias (at grips with his "faults" of style) and Saussure's (obsessed by the anagrammatical response to Latin and Greek lines of verse). And to end with: contrary to what one might expect, it is not polysemy (multiplicity of meaning) which is praised and sought out; it is quite precisely amphibology, duplicity; the fantasy is not to hear everything (anything), it is to hear *something else* (in this I am more classical than the theory of the text which I defend).

En écharpe ~ Aslant

On the one hand, what he says about the large objects of knowledge (cinema, language, society) is never memorable: the treatise (the article *on* something) is a kind of enormous falling off. Whatever pertinence there happens to be comes only in the margins, the interpolations, the parentheses, *aslant:* it is the subject's voice *off*, as we say, off-camera, off-microphone, offstage.

On the other hand, he never makes explicit (never defines) the notions which seem most necessary to him and which he constantly makes use of (constantly subsumed under a word). The *Doxa* is invariably allegated, but is not defined: no piece on the *Doxa*. The

73

Text is never approached except metaphorically: it is the field of the haruspex, it is a banquette, a faceted cube, an excipient, a Japanese stew, a din of decors, a braid, some Valenciennes lace, a Moroccan wadi, a broken television screen, a layered pastry, an onion, etc. And when he comes up with a treatise "on" the Text (for an encyclopedia), without denying it (never deny anything: in the name of what present?), it is a labor of knowledge, not of writing.

La chambre d'échos ~ The echo chamber

In relation to the systems which surround him, what is he? Say an echo chamber: he reproduces the thoughts badly, he follows the words; he pays his visits, i.e., his respects, to vocabularies, he *invokes* notions, he rehearses them under a name; he makes use of this name as of an emblem (thereby practicing a kind of philosophical ideography) and this emblem dispenses him from following to its conclusion the system of which it is the signifier (which simply makes him a sign). Coming from psychoanalysis and seeming to remain there, *"transference,"* nonetheless, readily leaves the Oedipal situation. The Lacanian *"image-repertory"*—*imaginaire*—extends to the borders of the classical "self-love"—*amour-propre.* *"Bad faith"* leaves the Sartrian system to join the critique of mythologies. *"Bourgeois"* receives the whole Marxist accent, but keeps overflowing toward the aesthetic and the ethical. In this way, no doubt, words are shifted, systems communicate, modernity is tried (the way one tries all the push buttons on a radio one doesn't know how to work), but the intertext thereby created is literally *superficial:* one adheres *liberally:* the name (philosophic, psychoanalytic, political, scientific) retains with its original system a line which is not cut but which remains: tenacious and floating. No doubt the reason for this is that one cannot at one and the same time desire a word and take it to its conclusion: in him, the desire for the word prevails, but this pleasure is partly constituted by a kind of doctrinal vibration.

Notes

in bed . . .

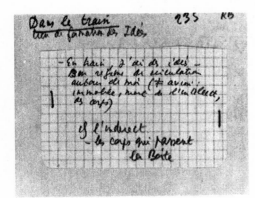

*Reversal: of scholarly origin, the note follows the
various twists and turns of movement.*

. . . outside . . .

. . or at a desk

L'écriture commence par le style ~ Writing begins with style

Sometimes he attempts to use the asyndeton so much admired by Chateaubriand under the name of anacoluthon: what relation can be found between milk and the Jesuits? The following: ". . . those milky phonemes which the remarkable Jesuit, van Ginnekin, posited between writing and language" (*The Pleasure of the Text*). Then there are the countless antitheses (deliberate, farfetched, corseted) and word play from which a whole system is derived (pleasure: *precarious* / bliss: *precocious*). In short, countless traces of the work of *style,* in the oldest sense of the word. Yet this style serves to praise a new value, *writing,* which is excess, overflow of style toward other regions of language and subject, far from a *classed* literary code (exhausted code of a doomed class). This contradiction may perhaps be explained and justified as follows: his way of writing was formed at a moment when the writing of the essay sought a renewal by the combination of political intentions, philosophical notions, and true rhetorical figures (Sartre is full of them). But above all, style is somehow the beginning of writing: however timidly, by committing itself to great risks of recuperation, it sketches the reign of the signifier.

À quoi sert l'utopie ~ What is a utopia for?

What is a utopia for? To make meaning. Confronting the present, my present, a utopia is a second term which permits the sign to function: discourse about reality becomes possible, I emerge from the aphasia into which I am plunged by the panic of all that doesn't *work* within me, in this world which is mine.

The utopia is familiar to the writer, for the writer is a bestower of meaning: his task (or his delight) is to give meanings, names, and he can do so only if there is a paradigm, functioning of the *yes/no* mechanism, alternation of the two values: for the writer, the world is a medal, a coin, a double surface of reading, his own reality occupying its reverse and the utopia the obverse. The Text, for example, is a utopia; its—semantic—function is to make the present literature, art, language signify, insofar as they are declared *impossible;* hitherto, literature was explained by its past; today, by its utopia: the meaning is based on value: the utopia permits this new semantics.

Revolutionary writings have always scantily and poorly represented the daily finality of the revolution, the way it suggests *we shall live tomorrow,* either because this representation risks sweetening or trivializing the present struggle, or because, more precisely, political theory aims only at setting up the real freedom of the human question, without prefiguring any of its answers. Hence utopia would be the taboo of the revolution, and the writer would be responsible for transgressing it; he alone could *risk* that representation; like a priest, he would assume the eschatological discourse; he would close the ethical circle, answering by a final vision of values to the initial revolutionary *choice* (the reason why one *becomes* a revolutionary).

In *Writing Degree Zero* (political) utopia has the (naïve?) form of a social universality, as if utopia could only be the strict converse of the present evil, as if division could only be answered, ultimately, by indivision; but subsequently, though vague and filled with difficulties, a pluralist philosophy has been appearing: hostile to "massification," tending toward difference, in short: Fourierist; whereupon a (still-maintained) utopia consists in imagining an infinitely fragmented society, whose division would no longer be social, and, consequently, no longer conflictive.

L'écrivain comme fantasme ~ The writer as fantasy

Surely there is no longer a single adolescent who has this fantasy: *to be a writer!* Imagine wanting to copy not the works but the practices of any contemporary—his way of strolling through the world, a notebook in his pocket and a phrase in his head (the way I imagined Gide traveling from Russia to the Congo, reading his classics and writing his notebooks in the dining car, waiting for the meals to be served; the way I actually saw him, one day in 1939, in the gloom of the Brasserie Lutétia, eating a pear and reading a

Matière

1. Plaisir certain.

2. Trop plein. Peur du vide.

3 Serpentin : trait bête qui
   signifie la volonté du hasard
   et non la pression du corps.
   Trait de bavardage.

4. Fantôme figuratif : oiseau,
   poisson des Îles.

book)! For what the fantasy imposes is the writer as we can see him in his private diary, *the writer minus his work:* supreme form of the sacred: the mark and the void.

Nouveau sujet, nouvelle science ~ New subject, new science

He wants to side with any writing whose principle is that *the subject is merely an effect of language.* He imagines an enormous science, in the utterance of which the scientist would at last include himself—the science of the effects of language.

Est-ce toi, chère Élise . . . ~ Is that you, Elise dear . . .

. . . does not in the least mean: I am ascertaining the doubtful identity of the person coming in by asking the very singular question: "Is she she?" but on the contrary means: you see, you hear, the person coming in is called—or rather will be called *Élise,* I know her very well, and you are entitled to assume that I am on splendid terms with her. And then this too: caught up in the very form of the utterance, there is the vague recollection of all the situations in which someone has said: *"Is that you?"* and even beyond, there is the blind subject in the process of interrogating *a woman who has come in* (and if it isn't you, what a disappointment—or what a relief), etc.

Is linguistics to concern itself with the message or with the language? That is, in this case, with the *web of meaning as it is spun out?* What are we to call this true linguistics, which is the linguistics of connotation?

He had written: "The text is (should be) that uninhibited person who shows his behind to the Political Father" (*Pleasure of the Text*). One critic pretends to believe that "behind" has been substituted for "ass" out of timidity. What happens to connotation here? A good little devil doesn't show his ass to Mme MacMiche, he shows her his behind; the childish word was necessary, since we were concerned with the Father. To read in any real way, then, is to enter into connotation. Futile maneuver: in dealing with the denoted meaning, positivist linguistics deals with a meaning so extenuated that it has become obscure, improbable, unreal; it disdainfully refers to a fantasy-linguistics the clear, the brilliant meaning, the meaning of the subject in the process of utterance (clear meaning? Yes, a meaning bathed in light, as in a dream, where I keenly perceive the anguish, the excess, the imposture of a situation, much more acutely than the story which is taking place there).

L'ellipse ~ Ellipsis

Someone questions him: "You wrote somewhere that *writing proceeds through the body:* can you explain what you meant?

He realizes then how obscure such statements, clear as they are to him, must be for many others. Yet the phrase is anything but meaningless, merely elliptical: it is an ellipsis which is not supported. To which may be added here a less formal resistance: public opinion has a reduced conception of the body; it is always, apparently, what is opposed to the soul: any somewhat metonymic extension of the body is taboo.

Ellipsis, a misunderstood figure, disturbs because it represents the dreadful freedom of language, which is somehow *without necessary proportion:* its modules are altogether artificial, entirely learned; I am no longer any more astonished by La Fontaine's ellipses (yet, how many unformulated relays between the grasshopper's song and her destitution) than by the physical ellipsis which unites in a simple piece of equipment both electric current and cold, because these shortcuts are placed in a purely operative field: that of academic apprenticeship and of the kitchen; but the text is not operative: there is no *antecedent* to the logical transformations it proposes.

L'emblème, le gag ~ Emblem, gag

What a textual treasury, *A Night at the Opera!* If some critical demonstration requires an allegory in which the wild mechanics of the text-on-a-spree explodes, the film will provide it for me: the

steamer cabin, the torn contract, the final chaos of opera decors—
each of these episodes (among others) is the emblem of the logical
subversions performed by the Text; and if these emblems are perfect, it is ultimately because they are comic, laughter being what,
by a last reversal, releases demonstration from its demonstrative attribute. What liberates metaphor, symbol, emblem from poetic
mania, what manifests its power of subversion, is the *preposterous,*
that "bewilderment" which Fourier was so good at getting into his
examples, to the scorn of any rhetorical respectability (*Sade,*
Fourier, Loyola). The logical future of metaphor would therefore be
the gag.

Une société d'émetteurs ~ A society of transmitters

I live in a society of *transmitters* (being one myself): each person I meet or who writes to me, sends me a book, a text, an
outline, a prospectus, a protest, an invitation to a performance, an
exhibition, etc. The pleasure of writing, of producing, makes itself
felt on all sides; but the circuit being commercial, free production
remains clogged, hysterical, and somehow bewildered; most of the
time, the texts and the performances proceed where there is no
demand for them; they encounter, unfortunately for them, "relations" and not friends, still less partners; so that this kind of collective ejaculation of writing, in which one might see the *utopian*
scene of a free society (in which pleasure would circulate without
the intermediary of money), reverts today to the apocalypse.

Emploi du temps ~ Schedule

"During vacation I get up at seven, go downstairs, and open
the house, make myself some tea, break up some bread for the
birds waiting in the garden, wash, dust my desk, empty its ash-
trays, cut a rose, listen to the seven-thirty news. At eight, my
mother comes downstairs too; I take breakfast with her: two soft-
boiled eggs, a slice of toast and black coffee, no sugar; at eight-
fifteen, I go for the paper in the village; I say to Mme C.: *A lovely*
day, overcast, etc.; and then I begin working. At nine-thirty, the

postman comes (*Sultry this morning, what a lovely day,* etc.), and a little later, in her delivery truck full of loaves, the baker's daughter (she's in school, no occasion to mention the weather); at ten-thirty sharp, I make myself some black coffee, I smoke the day's first cigar. At one, we have lunch; I nap from one-thirty to two-thirty. Then comes the moment when I drift: no will to work; sometimes I paint a little, or I go for some aspirin at the druggist's, or I burn papers at the back of the garden, or I make myself a reading stand, a file, a paper rack; by this time it is four, and I go back to work; at five-fifteen, it is teatime; around seven, I stop working; I water the garden (if it is good weather) and play the piano. After dinner, television: if the programs are too silly, I go back to my desk, and listen to music and take notes. I go to bed at ten and read a little from a couple of books: on the one hand, a work written in a highly literary language (Lamartine's *Confidences,* the Goncourts' *Journal,* etc.), on the other a detective novel (preferably an old one) or an (unfashionable) English novel, or some Zola.''

—All of which has no interest. Further, not only do you indicate your class allegiances, but you even make of such an indication a literary confession, whose *futility* is no longer welcome: you constitute yourself, in fantasy, as a "writer," or worse still: you *constitute yourself.*

Le privé ~ Private life

It is certainly when I divulge my *private life* that I expose myself most: not by the risk of "scandal," but because then I present my image-system in its strongest consistency; and the image-system, one's imaginary life, is the very thing over which others have an advantage: which is protected by no reversal, no dislocation. Yet "private life" changes according to the *Doxa* one addresses: if it is a *Doxa* of the right (bourgeois, petit bourgeois: institutions, laws, press), it is the sexual private life which exposes most. But if it is a *Doxa* of the left, the sexual exposition transgresses nothing: here "private life" is trivial actions, the traces of bourgeois ideology confessed by the subject: confronting this *Doxa,* I am less exposed in declaring a perversion than in uttering a taste:

passion, friendship, tenderness, sentimentality, delight in writing then become, by simple structural displacement, *unspeakable* terms: contradicting what can be said, what it is expected that you would say, but which precisely—the very voice of the image-system—you would like to be able to say *immediately* (without mediation).

En fait . . . ~ In fact . . .

You suppose that the goal of the wrestling match is to win? No, it is to understand. You suppose that the theater is fictive, ideal, in relation to life? No, in the photogeny of the d'Harcourt studios it is the stage which is trivial and the city which is dreamed. Athens is not a mythical city; it must be described in realistic terms, without reference to humanist discourse. The Martians? They are not invoked to stage the Other (the Alien) but the Same. The gangster film is not emotive, as might be supposed, but intellectual. Jules Verne a travel writer? Quite the contrary, a writer of claustration. Astrology is not predictive but descriptive (it describes very realistically certain social conditions). Racine's theater is not a theater of erotic passion but of authoritarian relations, etc.

Such figures of Paradox are countless; they have their logical operator: the expression *"in fact"*: striptease is not an erotic solicitation: *in fact* it desexualizes Woman, etc.

Éros et le théâtre ~ Eros and the theater

The theater (the particularized scene) is the very site of what used to be called *venusty*, charm, comeliness of form, i.e., of Eros observed, illuminated (by Psyche and her lamp). Enough that a secondary, episodic character offer some reason to be desired (this reason can be perverse, not attached to beauty but to a detail of the body, to the texture of the voice, to a way of breathing, even to some clumsiness), for a whole performance to be saved. The erotic function of the theater is not accessory, for the theater alone of all the figurative arts (cinema, painting) presents the bodies and not their representation. The body in the theater is at once contingent and essential: essential, you cannot possess it (it is magnified by the prestige of nostalgic desire); contingent, you might, for you would merely need to be momentarily crazy (which is within your power) in order to jump onto the stage and touch what you desire. The cinema, on the contrary, excludes by a fatality of Nature all transition to the act: here the image is the *irremediable* absence of the represented body.

(The cinema would be like those bodies which pass by, in summer, with shirts unbuttoned to the waist: *Look but don't touch,* say these bodies and the cinema, both of them, literally, *factitious.*)

Le discours esthétique ~ Aesthetic discourse

He attempts to compose a discourse which is not uttered in the name of the Law and/or of Violence: whose instance might be neither political nor religious nor scientific; which might be in a sense the remainder and the supplement of all such utterances. What shall we call such discourse? *erotic,* no doubt, for it has to do with pleasure; or even perhaps: *aesthetic,* if we foresee subjecting this old category to a gradual torsion which will alienate it from its regressive, idealist background and bring it closer to the body, to the *drift.*

La tentation ethnologique ~ The ethnological temptation

What pleased him in Michelet is the foundation of an ethnology of France, the desire and the skill of questioning historically—i.e., *relatively*—those objects supposedly the most natural: face, food, clothes, complexion. Elsewhere the population of Racine's tragedies, and that of Sade's novels, have been described as tribed, as closed ethnic groups whose structure must be studied. In his *Mythologies,* it is France itself which is ethnographed. Further, he has always loved the great novelistic cosmogonies (Balzac, Zola, Proust), so close to little societies. This is because the ethnological book has all the powers of the beloved book: it is an encyclopedia, noting and classifying all of reality, even the most trivial, the most sensual aspects; this encyclopedia does not adulterate the Other by reducing it to the Same; appropriation diminishes, the Self's certitude grows lighter. Finally, of all learned discourse, the ethnological seems to come closest to a Fiction.

Étymologies ~ Etymologies

When he writes *abject,* it means *to be rejected; amiable* means *that can be loved;* the *image* is an *imitation; precarious: that one may implore, sway; evaluation* is an *establishment of value; obligation,* a *ligature; definition,* a *tracing of a limit,* etc.

His discourse is full of words he cuts off, so to speak, at the root. Yet in etymology it is not the truth or the origin of the word which pleases him but rather the *effect of overdetermination* which it authorizes: the word is seen as a palimpsest: it then seems to me that I have ideas *on the level of language*—which is quite simply: to write (I am speaking here of a praxis, not of a value).

Violence, évidence, nature ~ Violence, evidence, Nature

He could not get away from that grim notion that true violence is that of the *self-evident:* what is evident is violent, even if this evidence is gently, liberally, democratically represented; what is paradoxical, what does not follow of itself, is less so, even if it is imposed arbitrarily: a tyrant who promulgated preposterous laws would all in all be less violent than the masses which were content to utter *what is self-evident, what follows of itself:* the "natural" is, in short, *the ultimate outrage.*

L'exclusion ~ Exclusion

Utopia (à la Fourier): that of a world in which there would no longer be anything but differences, so that to be differentiated would no longer mean to be excluded.

Walking through the Church of Saint-Sulpice and happening to witness the end of a wedding, he has a feeling of exclusion. Now, why this faltering, produced under the effect of the silliest of spectacles: ceremonial, religious, conjugal, and petit bourgeois (it was not a large wedding)? Chance had produced that rare moment in which the whole *symbolic* accumulates and forces the body to yield. He had received in a single gust all the divisions of which he is the object, as if, suddenly, it was the very *being* of exclusion with which he had been bludgeoned: dense and hard. For to the simple exclusions which this episode represented for him was added a final alienation: that of his language: he could not assume his distress in the very code of distress, i.e., *express it:* he felt more than excluded: *detached:* forever assigned the place of the *witness,* whose discourse can only be, of course, subject to codes of detachment: either narrative, or explicative, or challenging, or ironic: never *lyrical,* never homogenous with the pathos outside of which he must seek his place.

Céline et Flora ~ Céline and Flora

Writing subjects me to a severe exclusion, not only because it separates me from current ("popular") language, but more essentially because it forbids me to "express myself": *whom* could it express? Exposing the inconsistency of the subject, his atopia, dispersing the enticements of the imaginary, it makes all lyricism untenable (as the utterance of a central "emotion"). Writing is a dry, ascetic pleasure, anything but effusive.

Now, in the case of an erotic perversion, this dryness becomes lacerating: I am blocked, I cannot get into my writing the *enchantment* (pure image) of a seduction: how to speak of whom, to whom one loves? How to make the affect echo, except by relays so complicated that he will lose all its publicity, and hence all its joy?

This is a very subtle disturbance of language, analogous to the exhausting fadeout which, in a telephone conversation, affects only one of the speakers. Proust has described it very well—apropos of something quite different from love (is not the heterological example often the best?). When the aunts Céline and Flora want to thank Swann for his Asti wine, they do so by a series of farfetched allusions, excess of discretion, euphoria of language, an asteism so bewildering that no one understands them; they produce a discourse which is double but, unfortunately, not at all ambiguous, for the public face of it is somehow sanded down and rendered quite insignificant: communication collapses, not by unintelligibility, but because there functions a veritable schism between the (complimenting or amorous) subject's emotion and the nullity, the aphonia of his expression.

L'exemption de sens ~ Exemption of meaning

Evidently he dreams of a world which would be *exempt from meaning* (as one is from military service). This began with *Writing Degree Zero,* in which is imagined "the absence of every sign"; subsequently, a thousand affirmations incidental to this dream (apropos of the avant-garde text, of Japan, of music, of the alexandrine, etc.).

Curious that in public opinion, precisely, there should be a version of this dream; *Doxa,* too, has no love for meaning, which in its eyes makes the mistake of conferring upon life a kind of infinite intelligibility (which cannot be determined, arrested): it counters the invasion of meaning (for which the intellectuals are responsible) by the *concrete;* the concrete is what is supposed to resist meaning.

Yet for him, it is not a question of recovering a pre-meaning, an origin of the world, of life, of facts, anterior to meaning, but rather to imagine a post-meaning: one must traverse, as though the length of an initiatic way, the whole meaning, in order to be able to extenuate it, to exempt it. Whence a double tactic: against *Doxa,* one must come out in favor of meaning, for meaning is the product of History, not of Nature; but against Science (paranoiac discourse), one must maintain the utopia of suppressed meaning.

Le fantasme, pas le rêve ~ The fantasy, not the dream

Dreaming (whether nicely or nastily) is insipid (nothing so boring as the account of a dream!). On the other hand, fantasizing helps pass any interval of waiting, of insomnia; a kind of pocket novel you always carry with you and can open anywhere without anyone seeing anything, in the train, in the café, waiting for a rendezvous. The dream displeases me because one is entirely absorbed within it: the dream is *monologic;* and the fantasy pleases me because it remains concomitant to the consciousness of reality (that of the place where I am); hence is created a double space, disconnected, layered, at the heart of which a voice (I could never say which one, that of the café or that of the internal fable), as in the movement of a fugue, assumes a position of *indirection:* something is woven, *braided*—without pen or paper, there is an initiation of writing.

Un fantasme vulgaire ~ A vulgar fantasy

X once told me: "Can you conceive of the slightest frustration among Sade's libertines? And yet: even their unprecedented power, their prodigious freedom are weak compared to my own fantasy life. Not that I have any desire to add any particular practice to the apparently exhaustive list of their pleasures, but because the only freedom I can dream of is the one they don't have: the freedom to be able to take my pleasure of anyone I encounter and desire *instantaneously.* It's true," he added, "that this is a *vulgar* fantasy: am I not potentially the Sadist of the agony columns, the sex fiend who 'jumps' the passer-by in the street? In Sade, on the contrary, nothing ever suggests the mediocrity of newsprint."

Le retour comme farce ~ Recurrence as farce

Intensely struck, that first time, and struck forever by that notion of Marx's that in History tragedy sometimes recurs, *but as a farce.* Farce is an ambiguous form, since it permits us to read within it the figure of what it mockingly repeats: as with *Accountancy:* a positive value in the period when the bourgeoisie was a progressive force, a pejorative feature when that bourgeoisie had become triumphant, settled, exploitive; and as with the "concrete" (the alibi of so many mediocre scholars and dull politicians), which is merely the farce of one of the highest values: the exemption of meaning.

This farce recurrence is itself the mockery of the materialist emblem: the spiral (introduced by Vico into our Western discourse). On the spiral's trajectory, everything recurs, but in another, higher place: it is then the return of difference, the movement of metaphor; it is Fiction. Farce, however, recurs lower down; it is a metaphor which leans, fades, and falls (slackens).

La fatigue et la fraîcheur ~ Fatigue and freshness

The stereotype can be evaluated in terms of *fatigue*. The stereotype is what *begins* to fatigue me. Whence the antidote, cited as far back as *Writing Degree Zero:* the *freshness* of language.

In 1971, the expression "bourgeois ideology" had gone considerably sour and was beginning to "fatigue," like an old harness; he then undertook (discreetly) to write: "the *so-called* bourgeois ideology." Not that he denies this ideology its bourgeois stamp for a moment (quite the contrary: what else would it be?), but he must *denature* the stereotype by some verbal or graphic sign which displays its wear (quotation marks, for example). The ideal would of course be to erase, little by little, these external signs, while keeping the frozen word from returning to a state of nature; but to do this, the stereotyped discourse must be caught up in a *mimesis* (novel or theater): it is then the characters themselves who function as quotation marks: thus Adamov succeeds in his *Ping-Pong* in producing a language without display but not without distance: a *congealed* language (*Mythologies*).

(Doom of the essay, compared to the novel: doomed to *authenticity*—to the preclusion of quotation marks.)

In *Sarrasine,* La Zambinella declares that she seeks to be, for the sculptor who loves her, "a devoted friend" [*ami*], exposing, by this masculine form of the word, her true sex; but her lover fails to understand: he is abused *by the stereotype* (*S/Z*): how many times our universal discourse has used the expression "a devoted friend"! One would have to start with this half-grammatical, half-sexual apologia in order to recognize the *repression effects* of the stereotype. Valéry used to speak of those people who die in an accident because they are unwilling to let go of their umbrellas; how many subjects repressed, refracted, blinded as to their true sexuality, *because they are unwilling to let go of a stereotype.*

The stereotype is that emplacement of discourse *where the body is missing,* where one is sure the body is not. Conversely, in this supposedly collective text that I happen to be reading, sometimes the stereotype (*écrivance*) gives way and writing (*écriture*) appears; I am then sure that this piece of utterance has been produced by *one* body.

La fiction ~ Fiction

Fiction: slight detachment, slight separation which forms a complete, colored scene, like a decalcomania.

Apropos of style: "It is an image I want to interrogate, or more exactly a *vision:* how do we *see* style?" Perhaps every enterprise rests in this way on a *vision* of intellectual objects. Why should science not grant itself the right to have visions? (Quite often, luckily, it takes that right.) Could not science become fictional?

Fiction would proceed from a *new intellectual art* (which is how semiology and structuralism are defined in *Système de la Mode*). With intellectual things, we produce simultaneously theory, critical combat, and pleasure; we subject the objects of knowledge and discussion—as in any art—no longer to an instance of truth, but to a consideration of *effects.*

He would have wanted to produce not a comedy of the Intellect but its *romanesque,* its novelistic theory.

La double figure ~ The double figure

This work, in its discontinuity, proceeds by means of two

movements: the *straight line* (advance, increase, insistence of an idea, a position, a preference, an image) and the *zigzag* (reversal, contradiction, reactive energy, denial, contrariety, the movement of a *Z*, the letter of deviance).

L'amour, la folie ~ Love, madness

Order of the day, from Bonaparte, First Consul, to his guard: *"Grenadier Gobain has committed suicide for love: moreover he was a very fine soldier. This is the second event of this kind which has occurred within the corps in a month. The First Consul orders the guard to be notified: that a soldier must conquer the pain and melancholy of the passions; that there is as much true courage in suffering steadfastly the pangs of the soul as in standing fast under the fire of a battery . . ."*

From what language, one wonders, did these lovesick, melancholy grenadiers draw their passion (scarcely in accord with the image of their class and profession)? What books had they read—or what stories been told? Perspicacious of Bonaparte, identifying love with a battle, not—banally—because two partners confront one another, but because, cutting as rifle fire, the erotic explosion provokes bewilderment and fear: crisis, revulsion of the body, madness: a man who is in love in the romantic manner knows the experience of madness. Now, to such a madman, no modern word is given today, and it is ultimately for this reason that he feels himself to be mad: no language to usurp—except a very old one.

Anguish, wound, distress or jubilation: the body, from head to toe, overwhelmed, *submerged by Nature,* and all this nonetheless: *as if I were borrowing a quotation.* In the sentiment of love, in the erotic madness, if I would speak, I rediscover: Book, *Doxa,* Stupidity. Entanglement of language and the body: which begins?

Forgeries ~ Forgeries

How does it go, when I write?—Doubtless by movements of language sufficiently formal and repeated for me to be able to call them "figures": I divine that there are *figures of production,* text operators. Among others, these are: evaluation, nomination, amphibology, etymology, paradox, emphasis, enumeration, and here is another of such figures: *forgery* (in the jargon of graphologists, forgery is an imitation of handwriting). My discourse contains many coupled notions (*denotation/connotation, readerly/writerly*). Such oppositions are artifacts: one borrows from science certain conceptual procedures, an energy of classification: one steals a language, though without wishing to apply it to the end: impossible to say: this is denotation, this connotation, or: this passage is readerly, this writerly, etc.: the opposition is *struck* (like a coinage), but one does not seek to *honor* it. Then what good is it? Quite simply, it serves *to say something:* it is necessary to posit a paradigm in order to produce a meaning and then to be able to divert, to alter it.

This way of making a text go (by figures and operations) fits in well with the views of semiology (and of what subsists in semiology of the old rhetoric): it is thus historically and ideologically marked: my text is in fact *readerly:* I am on the side of structure, of the sentence, of the sentenced text: I produce in order to reproduce, as if I had a thought and represent it with the help of raw materials and of rules: *I write classic.*

Fourier ou Flaubert? ~ Fourier or Flaubert?

Who is more important historically: Fourier or Flaubert? In Fourier's work, there is virtually no direct trace of the History, agitated though it was, of which he was the contemporary. Whereas Flaubert narrates in the course of a novel all the events of 1848. Which does not keep Fourier from being more important than Flaubert: he has indirectly expressed the desire of History and it is in this that he is at once a historian and a modern: historian of a desire.

Le cercle des fragments ~ The circle of fragments

To write by fragments: the fragments are then so many stones on the perimeter of a circle: I spread myself around: my whole little universe in crumbs; at the center, what?

His first, or nearly first text (1942) consists of fragments; this choice is then justified in the Gidean manner "because incoherence is preferable to a distorting order." Since then, as a matter of fact, he has never stopped writing in brief bursts: the brief scenes of *Mythologies,* the articles and prefaces of *Critical Essays,* the lexias of *S/Z,* the fragments of the second essay on Sade in *Sade, Fourier, Loyola* and of *The Pleasure of the Text.*

He already regarded the wrestling match as a series of fragments, a sum of spectacles, for "in the ring, it is each moment which is intelligible, not duration" (*Mythologies*); with amazement and predilection he watched this sportive artifice, subject in its very structure to asyndeton and anacoluthon, figures of interruption and short-circuiting.

Not only is the fragment cut off from its neighbors, but even within each fragment parataxis reigns. This is clear if you make an index of these little pieces; for each of them, the assemblage of referents is heteroclite; it is like a parlor game: "Take the words: *fragment, circle, Gide, wrestling match, asyndeton, painting, discourse, Zen, intermezzo;* make up a discourse which can link them together." And that would quite simply be this very fragment. The index of a text, then, is not only an instrument of reference; it is itself a text, a second text which is the *relief* (remainder and asperity) of the first: what is wandering (interrupted) in the rationality of the sentences.

Never having done more in the way of painting than some *"tachiste"* daubing, I decide to begin a patient and regular apprenticeship in drawing; I try to copy a Persian composition of the seventeenth century ("Nobleman Hunting"); irresistibly, instead of trying to represent the proportions, organization, and structure, I copy and naïvely connect detail to detail; whence unexpected "conclusions": the horseman's leg turns out to be perched right on top of the horse's breastplate, etc. In other words, I proceed by addition, not by sketch; I have the antecedent (initial) taste for the detail, the fragment, the *rush,* and the incapacity to lead it toward a "composition": I cannot reproduce "the masses."

Liking to find, to write *beginnings,* he tends to multiply this pleasure: that is why he writes fragments: so many fragments, so many beginnings, so many pleasures (but he doesn't like the ends: the risk of the rhetorical clausule is too great: the fear of not being able to resist the *last word*).

Zen belongs to *torin* Buddhism, a method of abrupt, separated, broken openings (*kien* Buddhism is, conversely, the method of gradual access). The fragment (like the haiku) is *torin;* it implies an immediate delight: it is a fantasy of discourse, a gaping of desire. In the form of a thought-sentence, the germ of the fragment comes to you anywhere: in the café, on the train, talking to a friend (it arises laterally to what he says or what I say); then you take out your notebook, to jot down not a "thought" but something like a strike, what would once have been called a "turn."

Then if you put the fragments one after the next, is no organization possible? Yes: the fragment is like the musical idea of a song cycle (*La Bonne Chanson, Dichterliebe*): each piece is self-sufficient, and yet it is never anything but the interstice of its neighbors: the work consists of no more than an inset, an *hors-texte.* The man who has best understood and practiced the aesthetic of the fragment (before Webern) is perhaps Schumann; he called the fragment an "intermezzo"; he increased the intermezzi within his works as he went on composing: everything he produced was ultimately *intercalated:* but between what and what? What is the meaning of a pure series of interruptions?

The fragment has its ideal: a high condensation, not of thought, or of wisdom, or of truth (as in the Maxim), but of music: "development" would be countered by "tone," something articulated and sung, a diction: here it is *timbre* which should reign.

Webern's *small pieces:* no cadence: with what sovereignty he *turns short!*

Le fragment comme illusion ~ The fragment as illusion

I have the illusion to suppose that by breaking up my discourse I cease to discourse in terms of the imaginary about myself, attenuating the risk of transcendence; but since the fragment (haiku, maxim, *pensée,* journal entry) is *finally* a rhetorical genre and since rhetoric is that layer of language which best presents itself to interpretation, by supposing I disperse myself I merely return, quite docilely, to the bed of the imaginary.

Du fragment au journal ~ From the fragment to the journal

With the alibi of a pulverized discourse, a dissertation destroyed, one arrives at the regular practice of the fragment; then from the fragment one slips to the "journal." At which point, is not the point of all this to entitle oneself to write a "journal"? Am I not justified in considering everything I have written as a clandestine and stubborn effort to bring to light again, someday, quite freely, the theme of the Gidean "journal"? At the terminal horizon, perhaps quite simply the initial text (his very first text was concerned with Gide's *Journal).*

Yet the (autobiographical) "journal" is, nowadays, discredited. Change partners: in the sixteenth century, when they were beginning to be written, without repugnance they were called a *diary: diarrhea . . .*

Production of my fragments. Contemplation of my fragments (correction, polishing, etc.). Contemplation of my scraps (narcissism).

La fraisette ~ *La fraisette*

All of a sudden, the Woman in Charlus surfaced: not when he was cruising soldiers and coachmen, but when, at the Verdurins', he asked for a strawberry liqueur—asked, in a shrill voice, for some *fraisette*. Would drink be *a good head for reading* (a head in search of the body's truth)?

Drinks one drinks all one's life without really liking them: tea, whiskey. Drinks-for-times, drinks-for-effects, and not drinks-for-flavors. Search for an ideal drink: which would be rich in metonymies of all kinds.

The taste of good wine (the *straight* taste of wine) is inseparable from food. To drink wine is to eat. On dietetic pretexts, the manager of the T. gives the rule for this symbolism: If you drink a glass of wine before the meal is served, it should be accompanied by a piece of bread: so that a counterpoint, a concomitance is created: civilization begins with duplicity (overdetermination): is not a good wine the wine whose flavor oscillates, alters, doubles, so that the mouthful swallowed does not have quite the same taste as the next mouthful taken? In the draught of good wine, as in the taking of the text, there is a torsion, a twist of degrees: it turns back, like a lock of hair.

In recalling the little things he had been deprived of in his childhood, he found what he liked today: for instance, iced drinks (very cold beer), because in those days there were no refrigerators yet (the tap water, at B., in the heavy summers, was always tepid).

Français ~ French

French by fruits (as others were "by women"): a predilection for pears, cherries, raspberries; somewhat less for oranges; and none whatever for exotic fruits such as mangoes, guavas, lichee nuts.

Fautes de frappe ~ Typos

To type: no traces: nothing exists, and then all of a sudden the word is there: no approximation, no *production;* there is no birth of the letter, but the expulsion of a little scrap of code. Typos are therefore very special: faults of essence: mistaking the keys, I attack the system at its heart; the typo is never vague, *indecipherable*, but a legible mistake, a meaning. However, my whole body enters into these code mistakes: this morning, getting up too early by accident, I keep making mistakes, spoiling my copy, and I write another text (that drug, fatigue); and under normal circumstances, I always make the same mistakes: disorganizing, for instance, the "structure" by a persistent metathesis, or by substituting *z* (the bad letter) for *s* in plurals (in what I write by hand, I always make only one mistake, though a frequent one: I write *n* for *m*, amputating one leg—I want letters with two legs, not three). These mechanical errors, insofar as they are not skids but substitutions, therefore refer to an entirely different disturbance than manuscript particularities: through the machine, the unconscious writes much more surely than natural script does, and one can conceive of a *graphanalysis,* much more pertinent than our insipid graphology; it is true that a good secretary does not make mistakes: she has no unconscious!

Le frisson du sens ~ The thrill of meaning

It is evident that the object of all his work is a morality of the sign (*morality* is not *morale*).

In this morality, as a frequent theme, the thrill of meaning has a double place; it is that first state according to which the "natural" begins to stir, to signify (to become once again relative, historical, idiomatic); the (abhorred) illusion of the *self-evident* chips, cracks, the machine of languages starts up, "Nature" shudders with all the sociality compressed, sleeping, within it: I am astounded by the "natural" aspect of sentences, as Hegel's ancient Greek was astounded by Nature and in it heard the thrill of meaning. Yet to this initial state of semantic reading, according to which things are proceeding toward the "true" meaning (that of History), corresponds elsewhere and almost contradictorily another value: meaning, before collapsing into in-significance, shudders still: *there is meaning,* but this meaning does not permit itself to be "caught"; it remains fluid, shuddering with a faint ebullition. The ideal state of sociality is thereby declared: an enormous and perpetual rustling animates with countless meanings which explode, crepitate, burst out without ever assuming the definitive form of a sign grimly weighted by its signified: a happy and impossible theme, for this ideally thrilling meaning is pitilessly recuperated by a solid meaning (that of the *Doxa*) or by a null meaning (that of the mystiques of liberation).

(Forms of this thrill: the Text, significance, and perhaps: the Neuter.)

L'induction galopante ~ Galloping induction

Temptation of reasoning: from this, that the narrative of dreaming excludes its auditor (from the pleasures of its referent), to induce that one of the functions of Narrative would be to *exclude* its reader.

(Two imprudences: not only is the phenomenon not certain—how to ascertain that the telling of a dream is boring, except from a highly personal sentiment—but it is also exaggeratedly abstract, aggrandized to the general category of Narrative: this uncertain phenomenon becomes the starting point of an abusive extension. What carries all before it is the flavor of paradox: to be able to suggest that Narrative is not at all projective, to be able to subvert the narrative *Doxa*.)

Gaucher ~ Left-handed

To be left-handed—what does it mean? You eat contrary to the place assigned to the table setting; you find the grip of the telephone on the wrong side, when someone right-handed has used it before you; the scissors are not made for your thumb. In school, years ago, you had to struggle to be like the others, you had to normalize your body, sacrifice your good hand to the little society of the *lycée* (I was constrained to draw with my right hand, but I put in the colors with my left: the revenge of impulse); a modest, inconsequential exclusion, socially tolerated, marked adolescent life with a tenuous and persistent crease: you got used to it, adapted to it, and went on . . .

Les gestes de l'idée ~ Gestures of the idea

The Lacanian subject (for instance) never makes him think of Tokyo; but Tokyo makes him think of the Lacanian subject. This procedure is a constant one: he rarely starts from the idea in order to invent an image for it subsequently; he starts from a sensuous object, and then hopes to meet in his work with the possibility of finding an *abstraction* for it, levied on the intellectual culture of the moment: philosophy then is no more than a reservoir of particular images, of ideal fictions (he borrows objects, not reasonings). Mallarmé speaks of "gestures of the idea": he finds the gesture first (expression of the body), then the idea (expression of the culture, of the intertext).

Abgrund ~ *Abgrund*

Can one—or at least could one ever—begin to write without taking oneself for another? For the history of sources we should substitute the history of figures: the origin of the work is not the first influence, it is the first posture: one copies a role, then, by metonymy, an art: I begin producing by reproducing the person I want to be. This first want (I desire and I pledge myself) establishes a secret system of fantasies which persist from age to age, often independently of the writings of the desired author.

One of his first articles (1942) concerned Gide's *Journal;* the writing of another (*"En Grèce,"* 1944) was evidently imitated from *Les Nourritures terrestres.* And Gide occupied a great place in his early reading: a diagonal cross-breed of Alsace and Gascony, as Gide was of Normandy and Languedoc, Protestant, having a taste for "letters" and fond of playing the piano, without counting the rest—how could he have failed to recognize himself, to desire himself in this writer? The Gidean *Abgrund,* the Gidean core, unchanging, still forms in my head a stubborn swarm. Gide is my original language, my *Ursuppe,* my literary soup.

Le goût des algorithmes ~ The taste for algorithms

He has never worked out real algorithms; there was a moment when he fell back on less arduous formalizations (but this moment seems to have passed): what seemed to be simple equations, schemas, tables, genealogical trees. Such figures, in fact, are of no use whatever; they are simple toys, the analogue of the dolls made out of a corner of one's handkerchief: one plays *for oneself:* Zola, in the same way, makes himself a plan of Plassans to explain his novel to himself. Such diagrams, he knows, even fail to have the interest of locating his discourse under the aegis of scientific reasoning: whom could they deceive? Yet one plays at science, one puts it in the picture—like a piece in a collage. In the same way, *calculation*—from which *pleasure* was to be derived—was placed by Fourier in a phantasmatic series (for there are fantasies of discourse).

Et si je n'avais pas lu . . . ~ And if I hadn't read . . .

And if I hadn't read Hegel, or *La Princesse de Clèves,* or Lévi-Strauss on *Les Chats,* or *l'Anti-Œdipe?*—The book which I haven't read and which is frequently *told to me* even before I have time to read it (which is perhaps the reason I don't read it): this book exists to the same degree as the other: it has its intelligibility, its memorability, its mode of action. Have we not enough freedom to receive a text *without the letter?*

(Repression: not to have read Hegel would be an exorbitant defect for a philosophy teacher, for a Marxist intellectual, for a Bataille specialist. But for me? Where do my reading duties begin?)

The man who makes a practice of writing agrees cheerfully enough to diminish or to divert the acuity, the responsibility of his ideas (one must risk this in the tone one usually employs in saying: *What does it matter to me? don't I have the essentials?*): in writing there would be the pleasure of a certain inertia, a certain mental *facility:* as if I were more indifferent to my own stupidity when I write than when I speak (how often professors are more intelligent than writers).

Hétérologie et violence ~ Heterology and violence

He fails to explain to himself how he can (along with others) sustain a textual theory of heterology (hence of discontinuity) on

"Suivant moi, l'hypocrisie était impossible
en mathématique et dans ma simplicité juvénile, je
pensais qu'il en était ainsi dans toutes les sciences
où j'avais ouï dire qu'elles s'appliquaient." (Stendhal).

(même celles-là)

Nul, absolument, nul en maths et en
logique, il n'a jamais eu manié de véritables
algorithmes ; il s'est rabattu sur des formalisations
moins ardues : des ~~formules~~ des lettres/schémas,
des tables, des arbres. Les figures, à vrai dire, ne
servent à rien ni à personne ; ce sont des joujoux,
par compliqués [...] fait un plan
un mouchoir (Zola, de la sorte, se fait un plan
pour s'expliquer [lui même] son roman)
Ces dessins n'ont même pas l'intérêt de placer
le détour sous l'alibi scientifique : ils sont
[...] d'une imagerie décorative, [...] typogra-
phique [...] de la même façon, le calcul — dont
relevant le plaisir — était placé par Fourier
dans une chaîne fantasmatique (car il y a des
fantasmes de discours) (SFL. ▬ 99, 107).

(un jouet pour soi :

12 Juil

Corrections? More for the pleasure of studding the text

the one hand, and on the other keep projecting a critique of violence (without ever, it is true, developing it and assuming responsibility for it to the end). How can you be a fellow traveler with the avant-garde and its sponsors when you have an irenic preference for drifting?—Unless, in fact, it might not be worth the trouble, even at the price of a certain withdrawal, to act as if one glimpsed some *other style* of cleavage.

L'imaginaire de la solitude ∼ The image-system of solitude

He had always, up to now, worked successively under the aegis of a great system (Marx, Sartre, Brecht, semiology, the Text). Today, it seems to him that he writes more openly, more unprotectedly; nothing sustains him, unless there are still patches of bypassed languages (for in order to speak one must seek support from other texts). He says this without the infatuation which may accompany all declarations of independence, and without the pose of melancholy adopted to avow a solitude; but rather in order to account to himself for the feeling of insecurity which possesses him today and, still more perhaps, the vague torment of a *recession* toward the minor thing, the old thing he is when "left to himself."

—So you make a declaration of humility; you still don't escape the image-system for all that, and the worst kind of one: the psychological image-system. It is true that in doing so, by a reversal you had not foreseen and which you would readily overlook, you attest to the accuracy of your diagnostic: indeed, you *retrogress*.—But in saying as much, I escape . . . etc. (the ladder continues).

Hypocrisie? ∼ Hypocrisy?

Speaking of a text, he credits its author with not manipulating the reader. But he found this compliment by discovering that he himself does all he can to manipulate the reader, and that in fact he will never renounce an art of *effects*.

L'idée comme jouissance ~ Idea as delight

Public opinion does not like the language of intellectuals. Hence he has often been dismissed by an accusation of intellectualist jargon. And hence he felt himself to be the object of a kind of racism: they excluded his language, i.e., his body: "you don't talk the way I do, so I exclude you." Michelet himself (but the breadth of his thematics afforded him an excuse) had exploded against the intellectuals, the scribes, the clerks, assigning them to the region of *infra-sex:* a petit-bourgeois view which construes the intellectual, *on account of his language,* as a desexualized, i.e., devirilized, being: anti-intellectualism reveals itself as a protest of virility; at which point the only thing the intellectual can do, like Sartre's Genêt wanting to be and making himself the man he is dismissed as being, is to assume this language which is fastened on him from without.

And yet (a frequent trick of any social accusation), what is an idea for him, if not *a flush of pleasure?* "Abstraction is in no way contrary to sensuality" (*Mythologies*). Even in his structuralist phase, when the essential task was to describe the humanly *intelligible,* he always associated intellectual activity with delight: the *panorama,* for example—what one sees from the Eiffel Tower—is an object at once intellective and rapturous: it liberates the body even as it gives the illusion of "comprehending" the field of vision.

Les idées méconnues ~ Misunderstood ideas

We see one and the same critical idea (for instance: *Destiny is an intelligent design:* it falls *precisely* where it was not expected to fall) nourish one book (*On Racine*) and reappear much later in another (*S/Z*). So there are recurrent ideas: because he sets so much store by them (by virtue of what spell?). Now, these favorite ideas usually waken no echo. In short, it is *precisely* where I dare encourage myself to the point of repeating myself that the reader "drops" me (whereby—to revert—Destiny is indeed an intelligent design). In another way, I was glad to have published (assuming responsibility for the apparent silliness of the remark) that "one writes in order to be loved"; I am told that M.D. finds this sentence imbecilic: indeed, it is endurable only if consumed *to the third degree:* conscious of the fact that it has been first touching, then imbecilic, you are *finally* free to find it, perhaps, accurate (M.D. could not go that far).

La phrase ~ The sentence

The sentence is denounced as an ideological object produced as pleasure (a reduced essence of the Fragment). One can, then, either accuse the subject of contradiction or else induce from this contradiction an astonishment, even a critical return: and what if there were, as a second perversion, *a pleasure of ideology?*

Idéologie et esthétique ~ Ideology and aesthetic

Ideology: what is repeated and *consistent* (by this last adjective, it is excluded from the order of the signifier). So ideological analysis (or counter-ideology) need merely be repeated and consistent (by proclaiming *on the spot* its validity, by a gesture of pure clearance) in order to become, itself, an ideological object.

How escape this? One solution is possible: the *aesthetic* one. In Brecht, an ideological critique is not made *directly* (or else it would have once more produced a repetitive, tautological, militant discourse); it passes through aesthetic relays; counter-ideology creeps in by means of a fiction—not realistic but *accurate.* This is perhaps the role of the aesthetic in our society: to provide the rules of an *indirect and transitive* discourse (it can transform language, but does not display its domination, its good conscience).

X, to whom I say that his manuscript (a weighty tome attacking television) is too dissertative, insufficiently protected *aesthetically,* gives a start at this word and immediately gives me back as good as I gave: he has had many discussions of *The Pleasure of the Text* with his friends; my book, he says, "keeps brushing up against catastrophe." No doubt catastrophe, in his eyes, is to fall into the aesthetic.

L'imaginaire ~ The image-system

The image-system, total assumption of the image, exists in animals (though the symbolic does not), since they head straight for the trap, whether sexual or hostile, which is set for them. Does not this zoological horizon give the image-system a preponderance of interest? Is it not, *epistemologically,* a coming category?

The vital effort of this book is to stage an image-system. "To stage" means: to arrange the flats one in front of the other, to distribute the roles, to establish levels, and, at the limit: to make the footlights a kind of uncertain barrier. Hence it is important that the image-system be treated according to its degrees (the image-system is a matter of consistency, and consistency a matter of degrees), and there are, in the course of these fragments, several degrees of image-system. The difficulty, however, is that one cannot number these degrees, like the degrees of spirituous liquor or of a torture.

In earlier times, scholars sometimes discreetly followed a proposition with the corrective word *"incertum."* If the image-system constituted a clear-cut piece whose *embarrassment* was always certain, it would be enough to announce this piece on each occasion by some metalinguistic operator, in order to be cleared of having written it. This is what could be done here for some of the fragments (*quotation marks, parentheses, dictation, scene,* etc.); the subject, doubled (or *imagining himself* to be doubled), sometimes manages to sign his image-system. But this is not a sure-fire practice; first of all, because there is an image-system of lucidity and because by splitting up what I say, I merely project the image further along, in spite of everything, producing a secondary grimace; then and above all because, very frequently, the image-system creeps in stealthily, gently skating over a verb tense, a pronoun, a memory, in short, everything that can be gathered together under the very device of the Mirror and of its Image: *Me, myself, I.*

Hence the ideal would be: neither a text of vanity, nor a text of lucidity, but a text with uncertain quotation marks, with floating parentheses (never to close the parenthesis is very specifically: *to drift*). This also depends on the reader, who produces the *spacing* of the readings.

(At its full strength, the image-system is experienced thus: everything that I want to write about myself and that it embarrasses me *finally* to write. Or again: what cannot be written without the reader's indulgence. Now, each reader has his own indulgence; whence, provided one might classify these indulgences, it becomes possible to classify the fragments themselves: each one receives its image-system imprint from that very horizon where it supposes itself loved, unpunished, exempt from the embarrassment of being read by a subject without indulgence, or simply: *who would observe.*)

Le dandy ∼ The dandy

Lavish use of paradox risks implying (or quite simply: implies) an individualist position, and one may say: a kind of dandyism. However, though solitary, the dandy is not alone: S., himself a student, tells me—regretfully—that the students are individualists; in a given historical situation—of pessimism and rejection—it is the intellectual class as a whole which, if it does not become militant, is virtually a dandy. (A dandy has no philosophy other than a transitory one: a life interest: time is the time of my life.)

Qu'est-ce que l'influence? ∼ What is influence?

It is clear in the *Critical Essays* how the subject of the writing "evolves" (shifting from an ethic of commitment to an ethic of the signifier): he evolves according to the authors he treats, in order. The inducing object, however, is not the author I am talking about but rather *what he leads me to say about him:* I influence myself *with his permission:* what I say about him forces me to think as much about myself (or not to think as much), etc.

Hence there must be a distinction between the authors about whom one writes, and whose influence is neither external nor anterior to what one says about them, and (a more classical conception) the authors whom one reads; but what comes to me from the latter group? A kind of music, a pensive sonority, a more or less dense play of anagrams. (I had my head full of Nietzsche, whom I had just been reading; but what I wanted, what I was trying to collect, was a song of sentence-ideas: the influence was purely prosodic.)

L'instrument subtil ~ The subtle instrument

Program for an avant-garde:
"The world has surely become unhinged, and only violent movements can put it all back together. But it may be that among the instruments for doing so, there is one—tiny, fragile—which requires to be wielded delicately" (Brecht).

Pause: anamnèses ~ Pause: anamneses

At the afternoon snack, cold milk with sugar in it. At the bottom of the old white bowl there was a defect in the glaze; he never could tell if the spoon, as it turned, was touching this defect or a patch of sugar that had not dissolved or had not been washed.

Coming home from his grandparents' house on the streetcar, Sunday nights. Dinner was taken in the bedroom, beside the fire— soup and toast.

On the long summer evenings, the mothers strolled along the lanes, the children fluttering around them: holidays.

A bat came into the bedroom. Fearing it would get caught in her hair, his mother hoisted him up on her shoulders, they wrapped themselves in a bedsheet, and chased the bat with the fire tongs.

Straddling a chair at the corner of the Chemin des Arènes, Colonel Poymiro, purple-faced, the veins showing in his nose, mustachioed and myopic, at a loss for words, watched the crowd from the bullfight pass back and forth. What agony, what terror when the Colonel kissed him!

His godfather, Joseph Nogaret, occasionally would give him a bag of walnuts and a five-franc piece.

Mme Lafont, head of the lower school at the Bayonne lycée, always wore a suit, a shirtwaist, and a fox; as a reward for a good answer, she would give a bonbon in the shape and with the taste of a raspberry.

M. Bertrand, pastor in the rue de l'Avre, in Grenelle, spoke slowly, formally, his eyes closed. At each meal he would read a little out of an old Bible with a greenish linen cover embroidered with a cross. This would always last a long time—very long: on days when they were leaving, they thought they would miss the train.

A landau with two horses, ordered from Darrigrand, in the rue Thiers, came for the travelers once a year at the house, to take us to the Bayonne station, where we caught the night train for Paris. Waiting for the train, we played Yellow Dwarf.

The furnished apartment, rented by correspondence, was occupied. So there they were one November morning in Paris, in the rue de la Glacière, with their trunks and suitcases. The dairy woman next door took them in, and gave them hot chocolate and croissants.

In the rue Mazarine, you bought your magazines from a stationer who came from Toulouse; the shop smelled of frying potatoes; the woman came out of the back still chewing a last mouthful.

Very distinguished, M. Grandsaignes d'Hauterive, the fourth-form teacher, wielded a tortoiseshell lorgnette and smelled of pep-

per; he divided up the class into "camps" and "rows," each one with its "leader." All for contests about Greek aorists. (Why are old teachers such good "conductors" of memory?)

Around 1932, at Studio 28, one Thursday afternoon in May, alone, I saw Le Chien andalou; coming out at five in the afternoon, the rue Tholozé smelled of the café-au-lait the laundresses drank between batches of wash. Ineffable memory of displacement from an excess of insipidity.

In Bayonne, because of the huge trees in the garden, there were a lot of mosquitoes; there was netting at the windows (but it had holes in it). Little perfumed cones called Phidibus were burned to keep the mosquitoes away. Then came Fly-Tox, vaporized by a squeaking pump that was almost always empty.

The irritable M. Dupouey, first-form teacher, never answered a question he asked—sometimes he would wait for an hour in silence for someone to find the answer; or else he would send the student out of his classroom.

Summer mornings at nine, two little boys would wait for me in a modest, low house in the Beyris neighborhood; I had to help them do their vacation homework. Also waiting for me on a newspaper, prepared by a gaunt grandmother, was a goblet of very pale and very sweet café-au-lait, which turned my stomach.

Etc. (Not being of the order of Nature, anamnesis admits of an "etc.")

I call *anamnesis* the action—a mixture of pleasure and effort—performed by the subject in order to recover, *without magnifying or sentimentalizing it,* a tenuity of memory: it is the haiku itself. The *biographeme (Sade, Fourier, Loyola)* is nothing but a factitious anamnesis: the one I lend to the other I love.

These few anamneses are more or less *matte,* (insignificant:

exempt of meaning). The more one succeeds in making them *matte*, the better they escape the image-system.

Bête? ~ Stupid?

A classical view (based on the unity of the human person): stupidity is an hysteria: it would be enough to see oneself as stupid in order to be less so. A dialectical view: I agree to pluralize myself, to permit free cantons of stupidity to live within me.

Often he felt stupid: this was because he had only an *ethical* intelligence (i.e., neither scientific nor political nor practical nor philosophical, etc.).

La machine de l'écriture ~ The writing machine

Around 1963 (apropos of La Bruyère in *Critical Essays*) he worked up a great enthusiasm for the *metaphor/metonymy* opposition (though it had been familiar to him already, ever since his conversations with G., in 1950). Like a magician's wand, the concept, especially if it is coupled, *raises* a possibility of writing: here, he said, lies the power of saying something.

Hence the work proceeds by conceptual infatuations, successive enthusiasms, perishable manias. Discourse advances by little fates, by amorous fits. (The cunning of language: in French the word for this infatuation is *engouement,* which means an *obstruction:* the word remains in the throat, for a certain interval.)

À jeun ~ Fasting

When he made a date for the next rehearsal, Brecht would say to his actors: *Nüchtern!* Fasting! Don't fill up, don't gorge, don't be inspired, emotional, indulgent, be dry, as if you had fasted. —Am I sure I can endure what I write eight days later, *fasting?* This sentence, this idea (this sentence-idea), which pleases me when I find it, who is to say that *fasting* it won't turn my stomach? How to question my disgust (the disgust for my own failures)? How to prepare the best reading of myself I can hope for: not to love but only *to endure fasting* what has been written?

Lettre de Jilali ~ A letter from Jilali

"*I send my greetings, dear Roland. Your letter gave me great pleasure. Yet the latter affords the image of our intimate friendship which is in a sense without defects. On the other hand, I have the great joy to answer your serious letter and to thank you a thousand times and from the bottom of my heart for your splendid words. On this occasion, dear Roland, I shall speak to you of a disturbing subject (as I see it). The subject is as follows: I have a younger brother, a student in the third-form AS, a very musical boy (the guitar) and a very loving one; but poverty conceals and hides him in his terrible world (he suffers in the present, "as your poet says") and I am asking you, dear Roland, to find him a job in your kind country as soon as you can, since he leads a life filled with anxiety and concern; now you know the situation of young Moroccans, and this indeed astounds me and denies me all radiant smiles. And this astonishes you as well if you have a heart devoid of xenophobia and misanthropy. Awaiting your reply with impatience, I ask my God to keep you in perfect health.*"

(Delights of this letter: sumptuous, brilliant, literal and nonetheless immediately literary, literary without culture, every sentence emphasizing the pleasures of language, in all its inflections precise, pitiless, beyond any aestheticism but never—far from it—censuring the aesthetic (as our grim compatriots would have done), the letter speaks *at the same time* truth and desire: all of Jilali's desire (the guitar, love), all of the political truth of Morocco. This is precisely the utopian discourse one would want.)

Le paradoxe comme jouissance ~ Paradox as pleasure

G. comes out of a performance of Handke's play *The Ride Across Lake Constance* and in his excitement he describes what he has seen in these terms: *it's baroque, it's mad, it's kitsch, it's romantic*, etc. And, he adds, *it's completely dated!* For certain organizations, paradox is an ecstasy, then a loss—one of the most intense.

Addendum to *The Pleasure of the Text:* Bliss is not what *corresponds to* desire (what satisfies it) but what surprises, exceeds, disturbs, deflects it. One must turn to the mystics for a good formulation of what can cause the subject to deviate in this way: Ruysbroek: "I call intoxication of the mind that state in which pleasure exceeds the possibilities which desire had entertained."

(In *The Pleasure of the Text,* bliss is *already* said to be unforeseeable, and Ruysbroek's remark *already* cited; but I can always quote myself in order to signify an insistence, an obsession, since it is a matter of my body.)

Le discours jubilatoire ∼ Jubilatory discourse

"I love you, I love you!" Welling up from the body, irrepressible, repeated, does not this whole paroxysm of love's declaration conceal some *lack?* We would not need to speak this word, if it were not to obscure, as the squid does with his ink, the failure of desire under the excess of its affirmation.

Then are we forever doomed to the grim return of an *average* discourse? Is there no possibility that there exists in some forgotten corner of the logosphere the possibility of a pure jubilatory discourse? At one of its far edges—quite close, in fact, to mysticism—is it not conceivable that language should at last become the primary and somehow *insignificant expression* of a fulfillment?

There's no help for it: *I love you* is a demand: hence it can only embarrass anyone who receives it, except the Mother—and except God!

Unless I should be justified in flinging out the phrase in the (improbable but ever hoped-for) case when two *I love you*'s, emitted in a single flash, would form a pure coincidence, annihilating by this simultaneity the blackmail effects of one subject over the other: the demand would proceed to *levitate.*

ÉCOLE PRATIQUE
DES HAUTES ÉTUDES

(VIᵉ SECTION)
Sciences Économiques et Sociales

SORBONNE

17, Rue de la Sorbonne (ODÉon 24-13)

PARIS, le _____ 19

Squandering

Comblement ~ Fulfillment

All (romantic) poetry and music is in this demand: *I love you,
je t'aime, ich liebe dich!* But if by some miracle the jubilatory answer should be given, what might it be? What is the *taste* of fulfillment? Heine:

> *Doch wenn du sprichst: Ich liebe dich!*
> *So muss ich weinen bitterlich:*

I stagger, I fall, *I weep bitterly.* (Love's word has its work to perform—like a mourning.)

Le travail du mot ~ The word's work

And then, the scene changes: I conceive myself seeking a
dialectical way out of the maze. So I decide that the amorous apos-
trophe, though I repeat and rehearse it day by day through the
course of time, will somehow recover, each time I utter it, a new
state. Like the Argonaut renewing his ship during its voyage without changing its name, the subject in love will perform a long task
through the course of one and the same exclamation, gradually
dialecticizing the original demand though without ever dimming the
incandescence of its initial address, considering that the very task
of love and of language is to give to one and the same phrase
inflections which will be forever new, thereby creating an unheard-
of speech in which the sign's form is repeated but never is signified; in which the speaker and the lover finally triumph over the
dreadful *reduction* which language (and psychoanalytic science)
transmit to all our affects.

(Of the three image-systems I have just alleged, the last is the
most operative; for if an image is constructed, that image is at least
the image of a dialectical transformation—of a *praxis.*

La peur du langage ~ The fear of language

Writing a certain text, he experiences a guilty emotion of
jargon, as if he could not escape from a mad discourse no matter

how individual he made his utterance: and what if all his life *he had chosen the wrong language?* He is all the more readily overcome by this panic here (in U.) where, staying home at night, he watches television a good deal: here is continually represented (remonstrated) a public language from which he is separated; this language interests him, but this interest is not reciprocal: to the television public, his own language would seem entirely unreal (and outside of aesthetic delight, any unreal language is likely to be ridiculous). Such is the trajectory of language's energy: in a first impulse, to listen to the language of others and to derive a certain security from this distance; and in a second, to jeopardize this retreat: to be afraid of what one says (indissociable from the way in which one says it).

About what he has just written during the day, he has fears during the night. Night, fantastically, restores all the image-system of writing: the image of the *product,* the critical (or friendly) *gossip: it's too this, it's too that, it's not enough . . .* . At night the adjectives return, *en masse.*

La langue maternelle ∼ The mother tongue

Why so little enjoyment of, or so little talent for, foreign languages? English learned at the lycée (boring: Queen Mab, *David Copperfield, She Stoops to Conquer*). More pleasure in Italian, of which a former Milanese pastor (bizarre combination) taught him the rudiments. But of these languages he has never had more than a vaguely touristic command: he has never entered into a language: little taste for foreign literature, constant pessimism with regard to translation, confusion when confronted by the questions of translators, since so often they appear to be ignorant of precisely what I regard as the very meaning of a word: the connotation. All this jamming is the underside of his love for the mother tongue: the language of women. This is not a national love: on the one hand, he does not believe in the primacy of any one language and often experiences the cruel deficiencies of French; on the other, he never feels in a state of security in his own language; the occasions are frequent when he recognizes its threatening division; sometimes, listening to French people in the street, he is amazed to understand them, to share with them a part of his body. For doubtless the French language is nothing more or less for him than the umbilical language.

(And at the same time, a taste for the very exotic languages, such as Japanese, whose structure *represents* for him—image and remonstrance—the organization of an altogether different subject.)

Le lexique impur ~ The impure lexicon

Might he not be defined as follows: the dream of a pure syntax and the pleasure of an impure, heterological lexicon (which mingles the origin, the specialness of words)? This titration would account for a certain historical situation, but also for a datum of consumption: read a little more than the pure avant-garde but much less than an author of the high culture.

J'aime, je n'aime pas ~ I like, I don't like

I like: salad, cinnamon, cheese, pimento, marzipan, the smell of new-cut hay (why doesn't someone with a "nose" make such a perfume), roses, peonies, lavender, champagne, loosely held political convictions, Glenn Gould, too-cold beer, flat pillows, toast, Havana cigars, Handel, slow walks, pears, white peaches, cherries, colors, watches, all kinds of writing pens, desserts, unrefined salt, realistic novels, the piano, coffee, Pollock, Twombly, all romantic music, Sartre, Brecht, Verne, Fourier, Eisenstein, trains, Médoc wine, having change, *Bouvard and Pécuchet,* walking in sandals on the lanes of southwest France, the bend of the Adour seen from Doctor L.'s house, the Marx Brothers, the mountains at seven in the morning leaving Salamanca, etc.

I don't like: white Pomeranians, women in slacks, geraniums, strawberries, the harpsichord, Miró, tautologies, animated cartoons, Arthur Rubinstein, villas, the afternoon, Satie, Bartók, Vivaldi, telephoning, children's choruses, Chopin's concertos, Burgundian branles and Renaissance dances, the organ, Marc-Antoine Charpentier, his trumpets and kettledrums, the politico-sexual, scenes, initiatives, fidelity, spontaneity, evenings with people I don't know, etc.

I like, I don't like: this is of no importance to anyone; this, apparently, has no meaning. And yet all this means: *my body is not the same as yours.* Hence, in this anarchic foam of tastes and distastes, a kind of listless blur, gradually appears the figure of a bodily enigma, requiring complicity or irritation. Here begins the intimidation of the body, which obliges others to endure me *liberally,* to remain silent and polite confronted by pleasures or rejections which they do not share.

(A fly bothers me, I kill it: you kill what bothers you. If I had not killed the fly, it would have been *out of pure liberalism:* I am liberal in order not to be a killer.)

Structure et liberté ~ Structure and freedom

Who is still a structuralist? Yet he is one in this, at least: a uniformly noisy place seems to him unstructured because in this place there is no freedom left to choose silence or speech (how many times has he not said to someone beside him in a bar: *I can't talk to you because there's too much noise*). Structure at least affords me two terms, one of which I can deliberately choose and the other dismiss; hence it is on the whole a (modest) pledge of freedom: how on such a day can I give a meaning to my silence, since, *in any case,* I cannot speak?

L'acceptable ~ The acceptable

He frequently employs this linguistic notion: the *acceptable:* a form is acceptable (readerly, grammatical) when, in a given language, it can receive meaning. The notion can be transferred to the level of discourse. Hence the propositions of haiku are always "simple, common, acceptable" (*L'Empire des Signes*); hence again: from the mechanism of Loyola's *exercises* "emerges a coded, hence acceptable demand" (*Sade, Fourier, Loyola*); and in a general way, the science of literature (should it ever exist) will not have to prove any particular meaning, but to say "why a meaning is acceptable" (*Critique et Vérité*).

This virtually scientific notion (in that it is of linguistic origin) has its emotional side; it substitutes the validity of a form for its truth; and thereby, *surreptitiously,* one might say, it leads to the favorite theme of the disappointed, exempted meaning, or again: of a drifting availability. At this point, the *acceptable,* on the structural alibi, is a figure of desire: I desire the acceptable (readerly) form as a way of exorcising the double violence of overwhelming meaning and of heroic non-meaning.

Lisible, scriptible et au-delà ~ Readerly, writerly, and beyond

In *S/Z,* an opposition was proposed: *readerly/writerly.* A *readerly* text is one I cannot rewrite (can I write today like Balzac?); a *writerly* text is one I read with difficulty, unless I completely transform my reading regime. I now conceive (certain texts that have been sent to me suggest as much) that there may be a third textual entity: alongside the readerly and the writerly, there would be something like the *receivable.* The *receivable* would be the unreaderly text which catches hold, the red-hot text, a product continuously outside of any likelihood and whose function—visibly assumed by its *scriptor*—would be to contest the mercantile constraint of what is written; this text, guided, armed by a notion of the *unpublishable,* would require the following response: I can neither read nor write what you produce, but I *receive* it, like a fire, a drug, an enigmatic disorganization.

La littérature comme mathésis ~ Literature as mathesis

Reading classical texts (from *The Golden Ass* to Proust), he is always amazed by the sum of knowledge amassed and aired by the literary work (according to laws of its own, the study of which should constitute a new structural analysis): literature is a *mathesis,* an order, a system, a structured field of knowledge. But this field is not infinite: on the one hand, literature cannot transcend the knowledge of its period; and on the other, it cannot say everything: as language, as *finite* generality, it cannot account for objects, spectacles, events which would surprise it to the point of stupefying it; this is what Brecht sees when he says: "The events of Auschwitz, of the Warsaw ghetto, of Buchenwald certainly would not tolerate a description of literary character. Literature was not prepared for such events, and has not given itself the means to account for them."

Perhaps this explains our impotence to produce a realistic literature today: it is no longer possible to rewrite either Balzac, or Zola, or Proust, or even the bad socialist-realist novels, though their descriptions are based on a social division which still applies. Realism is always timid, and there is too much *surprise* in a world which mass media and the generalization of politics have made so profuse that it is no longer possible to figure it projectively: the world, as a literary object, escapes; knowledge deserts literature, which can no longer be either *Mimesis* or *Mathesis* but merely *Semiosis,* the adventure of what is impossible to language, in a word: *Text* (it is wrong to say that the notion of "text" repeats the notion of "literature": literature *represents* a finite world, the text *figures* the infinite of language: without knowledge, without rationale, without intelligence).

Le livre du Moi ~ The book of the Self

His "ideas" have some relation to modernity, i.e., with what is called the avant-garde (the subject, history, sex, language); but he resists his ideas: his "self" or ego, a rational concretion, ceaselessly resists them. Though consisting apparently of a series of "ideas," this book is not the book of his ideas; it is the book of the Self, the book of my resistances to my own ideas; it is a *recessive* book (which falls back, but which may also gain perspective thereby).

All this must be considered as if spoken by a character in a novel—or rather by several characters. For the image-repertoire, fatal substance of the novel, and the labyrinth of levels in which anyone who speaks about himself gets lost—the image-repertoire is taken over by several masks (*personae*), distributed according to the depth of the stage (and yet *no one—personne,* as we say in French—is behind them). The book does not choose, it functions by alternation, it proceeds by impulses of the image-system pure and simple and by critical approaches, but these very approaches are never anything but effects of resonance: nothing is more a matter of the image-system, of the imaginary, than (self-) criticism. The substance of this book, ultimately, is therefore totally fictive. The intrusion, into the discourse of the essay, of a third person who nonetheless refers to no fictive creature, marks the necessity of remodeling the genres: let the essay avow itself *almost* a novel: a novel without proper names.

La loquèle ∼ The gift of speech

On June 7, 1972, a strange condition: out of fatigue, nervous depression, an inner gift of speech overwhelmed me, a bombardment of sentences: which is to say, I feel both very intelligent and very futile.

This is entirely the contrary of writing, parsimonious in its very expenditure.

Lucidité ∼ Lucidity

This book is not a book of "confessions"; not that it is insincere, but because we have a different knowledge today than yesterday; such knowledge can be summarized as follows: What I write about myself is never *the last word:* the more "sincere" I am, the more interpretable I am, under the eye of other examples than those of the old authors, who believed they were required to submit themselves to but one law: *authenticity.* Such examples are History, Ideology, the Unconscious. Open (and how could they be otherwise?) to these different futures, my texts are disjointed, no one of them caps any other; the latter is nothing but a *further* text, the last of the series, not the ultimate in meaning: *text upon text,* which never illuminates anything.

What right does my present have to speak of my past? Has my present some advantage over my past? What "grace" might have enlightened me? except that of passing time, or of a good cause, encountered on my way?

It always comes down to this: what is the project of writing which will present, not the best pretense, but simply an *undecidable pretense* (as D. says of Hegel)?

Le mariage ~ Marriage

The relation to Narrative (to representation, to *mimesis*) has something to do with the Oedipus complex, as we know. But it also has something to do, in our mass societies, with marriage. Even more than the number of plays and films of which adultery is the subject, I see the sign of this in that (painful) moment of a TV interview: the actor J.D. is being questioned, "roasted," as to his relations with his wife (herself an actress); the interviewer *wants* this good husband to be unfaithful; this excites him, he *demands* an ambiguous phrase, the seed of a story. Thus marriage affords great collective excitations: if we managed to suppress the Oedipus complex and marriage, what would be left for us to *tell?* With them gone, our popular arts would be transformed entirely.

(Link between the Oedipus complex and marriage: a matter of having "it" and of transmitting "it.")

Un souvenir d'enfance ~ A memory of childhood

When I was a child, we lived in a neighborhood called Marrac; this neighborhood was full of houses being built, and the children played in the building sites; huge holes had been dug in the loamy soil for the foundations of the houses, and one day when we had been playing in one of these, all the children climbed out except me—I couldn't make it. From the brink up above, they teased me: lost! alone! spied on! excluded! (to be excluded is not to be outside, it is to be *alone in the hole,* imprisoned under the open sky: *precluded*); then I saw my mother running up; she pulled me out of there and took me far away from the children—against them.

Au petit matin ~ Early morning

An early-morning fantasy: all my life, I have dreamed of getting up early (a class desire: to get up early in order to "think," to write, not to take the commuter train); but I shall never see that early morning of my fantasy, even when I do get up early; for in order that it match my desire, it should have to turn out that no sooner up, without wasting a moment, I could see it in the lucidity, the consciousness, the accumulation of sensibility one has by the night's end. How to be *disposed* at will? The limit of my fantasy is always my *in-disposition*.

Méduse ~ Medusa

The *Doxa* is current opinion, meaning repeated *as if nothing had happened*. It is Medusa: who petrifies those who look at her. Which means that it is *evident*. Is it seen? Not even that: a gelatinous mass which sticks onto the retina. The remedy? As an adolescent I went swimming one day at Malo-les-Bains, in a cold sea infested with the kind of jellyfish we call medusas (what aberration led me to agree to swim there? I was one of a group, which justifies any cowardice); it was so ordinary to come out of the water covered with stings and blisters that the locker-room attendant phlegmatically handed you a bottle of potassium chloride as soon as you left the beach. In the same way, one might conceive of taking a (perverse) pleasure in the endoxal products of mass culture, provided that when you left the immersion of that culture, someone handed you on each occasion, as if nothing had happened, a little detergent discourse.

Queen and sister of the hideous Gorgons, Medusa was of a rare beauty with regard to the luster of her hair. Neptune having ravished and wed her in the temple of Minerva, the latter rendered her repulsive and transformed her hair into snakes.

(It is true that in the *Doxa's* discourse there are former beauties sleeping, the memory of a once-sumptuous and fresh wisdom; and it is indeed Athena, the wise deity, who takes her revenge by making the *Doxa* into a caricature of wisdom.)

Medusa, or the Spider: castration. Which *stuns* me, an effect produced by a scene I hear but do not see: my hearing is frustrated of its vision: I remain *behind the door*.

The *Doxa* speaks, I hear it, but I am not within its space. A man of paradox, like any writer, I am indeed *behind the door;* certainly I should like to pass through, certainly I should like to see what is being said, I too participate in the communal scene; I am constantly *listening to what I am excluded from;* I am in a stunned state, dazed, cut off from the popularity of language.

The *Doxa* is, as we know, oppressive. But can it be repressive? Let us read this terrible phrase from a revolutionary sheet (*La Bouche de Fer,* 1790): ". . . above the three powers must be placed a censorial power of surveillance and public opinion which will belong to all, and which all will be able to exercise without representation."

Abou Nowas et la métaphore ~ Abu Novas and metaphor

Desire is no respecter of objects. When a hustler looked at Abu Novas, Abu Novas read in his eyes not the desire for money but just desire—and he was moved by it. Let this serve as an apology for any and all sciences of displacement: the meaning transferred matters little or nothing, the terms of the trajectory matter little or nothing: the only thing that counts—and establishes metaphor—is *the transference itself.*

Les allégories linguistiques ~ Linguistic allegories

In 1959, apropos of the French presence in Algeria, you give an ideological analysis of the verb "to be." The "sentence," a grammatical object if ever there was one, permits you to say what happens in a Tangier bar. You keep the notion of "metalanguage," but in the category of image-reservoir. This is a constant procedure in your work: you use a pseudo-linguistics, a metaphorical linguistics: not that grammatical concepts seek out images in order to express themselves, but just the contrary, because these concepts come to constitute allegories, a second language, whose abstraction is diverted to fictive ends: the most serious of the sciences, the one which is responsible for the very being of language and supplies a whole portion of austere names, is *also* a reservoir of images, and as a poetic language enables you to utter what is strictly your desire: you discover an affinity between "neutralization," a notion which allows the linguists to explain very scientifically the loss of meaning in certain pertinent oppositions, and the *Neutral*, an ethical category which is necessary to you in order to erase the intolerable scar of the paraded meaning, of the oppressive meaning. And meaning itself—when you watch it functioning, you do so with the almost puerile amusement of a buyer who never tires of pulling the switch of some gadget.

Migraines ~ Migraines

I have got into the habit of saying *migraines* for *headaches* (perhaps because the word is so lovely). This unsuitable word (for it is not only half of my head which gives me pain) is a socially accurate one: mythological attribute of bourgeois woman and of the man of letters, the migraine is a class phenomenon: who ever heard of the proletarian or the small businessman with migraines? The social division occurs within my body: my body itself is social.

Why, in the country (in the southwest of France), should I have stronger and more frequent migraines? I am resting, in the open air, and yet more migrainous than ever. What am I repressing? My mourning for the city? The recurrence of my Bayonnais past? The boredom of childhood? Of what displacements are my migraines the trace? But maybe the migraine is a perversion? When I have a headache, perhaps it means that I am a victim of a partial desire, as if I were fetishizing a specific point of my body: *the in-*

side of my head: does it mean, then, that I am in an unhappy/amorous relation with my work? A way of dividing myself, of desiring my work and at the same time of being afraid of it?

So different from Michelet's migraines, "amalgams of bewilderment and nausea," my migraines are matte. To have a (never very strong) headache is for me a way of rendering my body opaque, stubborn, thick, *fallen,* which is to say, ultimately (back to the major theme) *neutral.* Absence of migraine, the insignificant vigilance of the body, coenesthesia degree zero—I should read these in short as the *theater* of health; in order to assure myself that my body is not healthy in an hysterical fashion, I should occasionally need to take away its *sign* of transparence and experience it as a kind of glaucous organ, rather than as a triumphant figure. Hence migraine would be a psychosomatic (and no longer a neurotic) affliction by which I should agree to enter—though *just a little way* (for the migraine is a tenuous thing)—into man's mortal disease: insolvency of symbolization.

Le démodé ~ The unfashionable

Subtracted from the book, his life was continuously that of an unfashionable subject: when he was in love (by the manner and the very fact), he was unfashionable; when he loved his mother (what would it have been if he had really known his father and by some misfortune had loved him too!), he was unfashionable; when he felt himself to be a democrat, he was unfashionable, etc. But suppose Fashion were to make an additional turn of the screw, then this would be a kind of psychological kitsch, so to speak.

La mollesse des grands mots ~ Limpness of important words

In what he writes there are two kinds of important words. Some are simply ill used: vague, insistent, they serve to take the place of several signifieds ("Determinism," "History," "Nature"). I feel the limpness of these important words, limp as Dali's watches. The others ("writing," "style") are remodeled according to a personal project, and these are words whose meaning is idiolectal. Though from the viewpoint of a "healthy editorial policy," these two categories do not have the same value, they nonetheless communicate: in the (intellectually) vague word, there is, and all the more intensely, an existential specification: *History* is a moral notion; it allows us to relativize the natural and to believe in a meaning of time; *Nature* is sociality in its oppressive, motionless aspect, etc. Each word *turns,* either like milk, spoiled in the disintegrated space of phraseology, or else like a tendril, down to the neurotic root of the subject. And other words, finally, are cruisers: they follow what they meet up with: *imaginary,* in 1963, is no more than a vaguely Bachelardian term; but by 1970—in *S/Z*—it has been rebaptized, transformed (even deformed) into the Lacanian version.

Le mollet de la danseuse ~ The dancer's calf

Granted that *vulgarity* is a breach in discretion, writing constantly risks being vulgar. Our writing (these days) develops within a language space which is still rhetorical and which cannot abandon being so, if we seek to be able (to any degree) to communicate (to be accessible to interpretation, to analysis). Writing therefore supposes certain *effects of discourse;* when certain of these effects are forced, writing becomes vulgar: each time, so to speak, it shows its *dancer's calf.* (The very title of this fragment is *vulgar.*)

The imaginary—the image-repertoire—grasped, immobilized within the writer's obsession, as though by the effect of a photographic snapshot, becomes a kind of *grimace;* but if the pose is deliberate, the grimace changes meaning (problem: how to tell?).

Politique / morale ~ Politics / ethics

All my life, politically, I have given myself a bad time. From which I infer that the only Father I have known (have granted myself) has been the political Father.

It is a *simple* thought which frequently occurs to me, but which I never see stated (it may be a *stupid* thought): Is there not always something ethical in the political? Is it not Value that establishes the political, the order of reality, pure science of social reality? In the name of what does a militant decide to . . . militate? Though wrenched away from any ethic, any psychology, does not political praxis have a . . . psychological and an ethical origin?

(This is a literally *retarded* notion, for by coupling Ethics and Politics, you are about two hundred years old, you date from 1795, the year when the Convention created the Academy of Political and Ethical Sciences: old categories, old nonsense. —But where is all this *false?* —Not *even* false; it is no longer the case, no longer current; ancient coins are not false, either; they are museum pieces, kept for a special consumption, the consumption of what is old. —But can't we get a little useful metal out of that old coinage? —What is useful in this stupid thought is to recognize in it intractable confrontation, the impact of two epistemologies: Marxism and Freudianism.)

Mot-mode ~ Fashion-word

He is not very good at getting to the heart of things. A word, a figure of thought, a metaphor, in short, a form fastens upon him for several years, he repeats it, uses it everywhere (for instance, "body," "difference," "Orpheus," "Argo," etc.), but he makes no effort to reflect further as to what he means by such words or such figures (and were he to do so, it would be to find new metaphors instead of explanations): you cannot get to the heart of a refrain; you can only substitute another one for it. And this, after all, is what Fashion does. In other words, he has his internal, his personal fashions.

Mot-valeur ~ Value-word

The favorite words he uses are often grouped by oppositions; of the two words of the pair, he is *for* one, *against* the other:

The History of Semiology

production/product, structuration/structure, systematics/system, poetics/poetry, copy/analogy, plagiarism/pastiche, figuration/representation, appropriation/property, model/plan, subversion/contestation, intertext/context, eroticization/erotics, etc. Sometimes it is not only a matter of oppositions (between two words) but of cleavages (within a single word): *automobile* is favored as behavior but frowned on as an object; the *actor* is saved if he participates in an anti-Physis but doomed if he belongs to pseudo-Physis; *artifice* is desired if it is Baudelairean (specifically opposed to Nature), depreciated as *ersatz* (pretending to mimic that very Nature). Thus between words, and even within words, passes what he calls, in *The Pleasure of the Text*, "the knife of Value."

Mot-couleur ~ Color-word

When I buy colors, it is by the mere sight of their name. The name of the color (*Indian yellow, Persian red, celadon green*) outlines a kind of generic region within which the exact, special effect of the color is unforeseeable; the name is then the promise of a pleasure, the program of an operation: there is always a certain *future* in the complete names. Similarly, when I say that a word is beautiful, when I use it because I like it, it is never by virtue of its sonorous charm or of the originality of its meaning, or of a "poetic" combination of the two. The word transports me because of the notion that *I am going to do something with it:* it is the thrill of a future praxis, something like an *appetite*. This desire makes the entire motionless chart of language vibrate.

Mot-mana ~ Mana-word

In an author's lexicon, will there not always be a word-as-mana, a word whose ardent, complex, ineffable, and somehow sacred signification gives the illusion that by this word one might answer for everything? Such a word is neither eccentric nor central; it is motionless and carried, floating, never *pigeonholed*, always atopic (escaping any topic), at once remainder and supplement, a signifier taking up the place of every signified. This word has gradually appeared in his work; at first it was masked by the instance of Truth (that of history), then by that of Validity (that of systems and structures); now it blossoms, it flourishes; this word-as-mana is the word "body."

Let mot transitionnel ~ The transitional word

How does the word become value? At the level of the body. The theory of this carnal word was given in his *Michelet:* this historian's vocabulary, the array of his value-words, is organized by a physical thrill, the taste or distaste for certain historical bodies. Thus he creates, by the interposition of a variable complication, certain "favorite" words, "favorable" words (in the magical sense of the adjective), "marvelous" words (brilliant and felicitous). These are "transitional" words, analogous to those pillow corners and pieces of the sheet which the child stubbornly sucks. As for the child, these favorite words constitute a part of his arena; and like transitional objects, they are of uncertain status; actually it is a kind of absence of the object, of meaning, that they *stage:* despite the hardness of their contours, the strength of their repetition, they are vague, floating words; they are trying to become fetishes.

Le mot moyen ~ The medium word

When talking, I am not sure of looking for *le mot juste;* rather, I try to avoid the stupid word. But since I feel some remorse for renouncing the truth too soon, I settle for *the medium word*.

Le naturel ~ The natural

The illusion of the natural is constantly denounced (in *Mythologies,* in *Système de la Mode;* even in *S/Z,* where it is said that denotation is reversed into the nature of language). The natural is never an attribute of physical Nature; it is the alibi paraded by a social majority: the natural is a legality. Whence the critical necessity of making the law appear under such "natural" appearances and, according to Brecht's phrase, "under the rule, the abuse."

We might see the origin of such a critique in the minority situation of R.B. himself; he has always belonged to some minority, to some margin—of society, of language, of desire, of profession, and even of religion (it was not a matter of indifference to be a Protestant in a class of Catholic children); in no way a severe situation, but one which somewhat marks the whole of social existence: who does not feel how *natural* it is, in France, to be Catholic, married, and properly accredited with the right degrees? The slightest deficiency introduced into this array of public conformities forms a kind of tenuous wrinkle in what might be called the social litter.

Against this "natural," I can rebel in two ways: by arguing, like a jurist, against a law elaborated without me and against me (*"I too am entitled to . . ."*), or by wrecking the majority's Law by a transgressive avant-garde action. But he seems to remain strangely at the intersection of these two rejections: he has complicities of transgression and individualist moods. This produces a philosophy of the anti-Nature which remains rational, and the *Sign* is an ideal object for such a philosophy: for it is possible to denounce and/or celebrate its arbitrariness; it is possible to enjoy the codes even while nostalgically imagining that someday they will be abolished: like an intermittent *outsider,* I can enter into or emerge from the burdensome sociality, depending on my mood—of insertion or of distance.

Neuf / nouveau ~ Neuf / nouveau

His partiality (the choice of his values) seems to him productive when the French language happens to provide him pairs of words at once close to each other and different, one of which refers to what he likes and the other to what he dislikes, as if one and the same vocable were to cover the semantic field and with a whisk of its tail were to reverse itself completely (it is always the same structure: the structure of the paradigm, which is in fact that of his desire). Hence with *neuf/nouveau: "nouveau"* is good, it is the felicitous movement of the Text: novation is historically justified in every society where regression threatens because of the regime; but *"neuf"* is bad: one must struggle with a "new" garment of this kind in order to wear it: *"neuf,"* the new, sits awkwardly, opposes the body because it suppresses the body's play, of which a certain worn quality is the guarantee: a *nouveau* which is not entirely *neuf*—that would be the ideal state of the arts, of texts, and of garments.

Le neutre ~ The neutral

The Neutral is not an average of active and of passive; rather it is a back-and-forth, an amoral oscillation, in short, one might say, the converse of an antinomy. As value (proceeding from the region Passion), the Neutral would correspond to the force by which social praxis sweeps away and renders unreal the scholastic antinomies (Marx, quoted in *On Racine:* "It is only in social existence that such antinomies as subjectivism and objectivism, spiritualism and materialism, activity and passivity, lose their antinomic character . . .")

Figures of the Neutral: white writing, exempt from any literary theater—Adamic language—delectable insignificance—the smooth—the empty, the seamless—Prose (a political category described by Michelet)—discretion—the vacancy of the "person," if not annulled at least rendered irretrievable—absence of *imago*—the suspension of judgment, of due process—displacement—the refusal "to keep oneself in countenance" (the refusal of any countenance whatever)—the principle of delicacy—drifting—pleasure in its ecstatic aspect: whatever avoids or thwarts or ridicules ostentation, mastery, intimidation.

No Nature. In a first period, everything comes down to the struggle between a *pseudo-Physis* (*Doxa,* the natural, etc.) and an *anti-Physis* (all my personal utopias): one is to be hated, the other to be desired. Yet, in some later period, this very struggle seems too theatrical to him; it is then, surreptitiously, repulsed, distanced by the defense (the desire) of the Neutral. The Neutral is therefore not the third term—the zero degree—of an opposition which is both semantic and conflictual; it is, *at another link of the infinite chain of language,* the second term of a new paradigm, of which violence (combat, victory, theater, arrogance) is the primary term.

Actif / passif ~ Active / passive

Virile / non-virile: this famous pair, which rules over the entire *Doxa,* sums up all the ploys of alternation: the paradigmatic play of meaning and the sexual game of ostentation (every well-formed meaning is an ostentation: copulation and execution).

As he said in an article of 1971, "What is difficult is not to liberate sexuality according to a more or less libertarian project but to release it from meaning, including from transgression as meaning. Consider the Arab countries. Here certain rules of 'good' sexuality are readily transgressed by an open practice of homosexuality . . . but this transgression remains implacably subject to a regime in the strict sense: homosexuality, a transgressive practice, then immediately reproduces within itself . . . the purest paradigm imaginable, that of *active/passive,* of *possessor/possessed, buggerer/buggeree . . .*" In such countries, then, the alternative is pure, systematic; it knows no neutral or complex term, as if it were impossible to conceive, with regard to this relation of exclusion (*aut . . . aut*), extra-polar terms. Now, this alternative is verbalized, above all, by bourgeois or petit bourgeois boys who, located in the field of promotion, need a discourse both *sadistic* (anal) and clear (buttressed on meaning); they want a pure paradigm of meaning and of sex, without a leak, without a flaw, without any overflow toward the margins.

Nonetheless, once the alternative is rejected (once the paradigm is blurred) utopia begins: meaning and sex become the object of a free play, at the heart of which the (polysemant) forms and the (sensual) practices, liberated from the binary prison, will achieve a state of infinite expansion. Thus may be born a Gongorian text and a happy sexuality.

L'accommodation ~ Accommodation

When I read, I *accommodate:* not only the crystalline humor of my eyes, but also that of my intellect, in order to reach the right level of signification (the one which suits me). A responsible linguistics must no longer be concerned with "messages" (to hell with "messages"!) but with these accommodations, which doubtless proceed by levels and thresholds: each of us *curbs* his mind, or *curves* it, like an eye, in order to grasp in the mass of the text *that certain intelligibility* he needs in order to know, to take pleasure, etc. In this, reading is a kind of work, a labor: there is a muscle which curves it.

It is only when it looks into infinity that the normal eye has no need to accommodate. Similarly, if I could read a text *to infinity,* I should no longer have any need to curb or to curve anything within myself. Which is what happens postulatively in the presence of the so-called avant-garde text (do not try, in this case, to accommodate: you will see nothing at all).

Le numen ~ The numen

Predilection for Baudelaire's phrase, quoted several times (notably apropos of wrestling matches): "the emphatic truth of gesture in the great circumstances of life." He called this excess of pose the *numen* (which is the silent gesture of the gods pronouncing on human fate). The *numen* is hysteria frozen, eternalized, trapped, since it is at last held motionless, pinioned by a long stare. Whence my interest in poses (provided they are framed), noble paintings, pathetic scenes, eyes raised to heaven, etc.

Passage des objets dans le discours ~ Movement of objects into discourse

Different from the "concept" and from the "notion," which are purely ideal, the *intellectual object* is created by a kind of leverage upon the signifier: once I *take seriously* such forms as an etymology, a derivation, a metaphor, I can create a kind of *word-*

thought for myself which will ferret through all my language. This word-object is both *vested* (desired) and *superficial* (employed, not explored); it has a ritual existence; as if, at a certain moment, I had *baptized* it with my sign.

It is a good thing, he thought, that out of consideration for the reader, there should pass through the essay's discourse, from time to time, a sensual object (as in *Werther,* where suddenly there appear a dish of green peas cooked in butter and a peeled orange separated into sections). A double advantage: sumptuous appearance of a materiality and a distortion, a sudden gap wedged into the intellectual murmur.

Michelet gave him his example: what relation between the anatomical discourse and the camellia blossom? —"The brain of a child," Michelet says, "is nothing but the milky blossom of a camellia." Whence, no doubt, the habit of *diverting himself,* as he writes, by unusual enumerations. Is there not a kind of voluptuous pleasure in inserting, like a perfumed dream, into a sociological analysis, "wild cherries, cinnamon, vanilla, and sherry, Canadian tea, lavender, bananas"? to relieve the burden of a semantic demonstration by the vision of "wings, tails, crests, plumes, tufts of hair, scarves, smoke, balloons, belts, and veils" out of which Erté forms the letters of his alphabet—or again, to introduce into a sociological journal "brocade trousers, capes, and the long white nightshirts" worn by hippies? Once you let a "bluish circle of smoke" into critical discourse, you can find the courage, quite simply . . . *to copy it over.*

(Thus, sometimes, in Japanese haiku, the line of written words suddenly opens and there is the drawing of Mount Fuji or of a sardine which delicately appears in place of the abandoned word.)

Odeurs ~ Odors

In Proust, three senses out of five conduct memory. But for me, setting aside the voice, less a matter of sound, actually, than by its texture of *perfume,* memory, desire, death, the impossible return are not to be found here; my body does not consent to the story

135

of the madeleine, the cobblestones, and the Balbec napkins. Of what will never return, it is odor which returns for me. As with the odor of my childhood in Bayonne: like the world encircled by the mandala, all Bayonne is caught up in a composite odor: that of Petit-Bayonne (the neighborhood between the Nive and the Adour): the rope used by the sandal makers, the dim grocery shop, the wax of the old wood, the airless staircases, the black of the old Basque women, black to the cloth cap holding their braided hair, Spanish oil, the dampness of the artisans' workshops (bookbinders, hardwares), the dust in the municipal library (where I learned about sexuality from Suetonius and Martial), the glue of pianos being repaired at Bossière's shop, a certain aroma of chocolate, a city product, all this consistent, historical, provincial, and southern.

(I recall odors with a certain mad intensity: because I am growing old.)

De l'écriture à l'oeuvre ~ From writing to the work

Snare of infatuation: to suggest that he is willing to consider what he writes as a work, an *"oeuvre"*—to move from the contingency of writings to the transcendence of a unitary, sacred product. The word *"oeuvre"* is already a part of the image-repertoire.

The contradiction is one between writing and the work (as for the Text, that is a magnanimous word: it shows no partiality to this difference). I delight continuously, endlessly, in writing as in a perpetual production, in an unconditional dispersion, in an energy of seduction which no legal defense of the subject I fling upon the page can any longer halt. But in our mercantile society, one must end up with a work, an *"oeuvre"*: one must construct, i.e., *complete,* a piece of merchandise. While I write, the writing is thereby at every moment flattened out, banalized, made guilty by the work to which it must eventually contribute. How to write, given all the snares set by the collective image of the work? —Why, *blindly.* At every moment of the effort, lost, bewildered, and driven, I can only repeat to myself the words which end Sartre's *No Exit:* Let's go on.

Writing is that *play* by which I turn around as well as I can in a narrow place: I am wedged in, I struggle between the hysteria necessary to write and the image-repertoire, which oversees, controls, purifies, banalizes, codifies, corrects, imposes the focus (and the vision) of a social communication. On the one hand I want to be desired and on the other not to be desired: hysterical and obsessional at one and the same time.

And yet: the closer I come to the work, the deeper I descend into writing; I approach its unendurable depth; a desert is revealed; there occurs—fatal, lacerating—a kind of *loss of sympathy:* I no longer feel myself to be *sympathetic* (to others, to myself). It is at this point of contact between the writing and the work that the hard truth appears to me: *I am no longer a child.* Or else, is it the *ascesis* of pleasure which I am discovering?

"On le sait" ~ "As we know"

An apparently expletive expression ("as we know," "it is well known that . . .") is put at the start of certain developments: he ascribes to current opinion, to common knowledge, the proposition from which he will start out: his endeavor is to react against a banality. And often what he must oppose is not the banality of common opinion but his own; the discourse which comes to him initially is banal, and it is only by struggling against that original banality that, gradually, he writes. Suppose he is to describe his situation in a Tangier bar—what he first manages to say is that the place is the site of an "interior language": a fine discovery! He then attempts to get rid of this importuning banality and to fish out of it some fragment of an idea with which he might have some relation of desire: the Sentence! Once this object is named, everything is saved; whatever he writes (this is not a question of performance), it will always be a vested discourse, in which the body will make its appearance (banality is discourse without body).

In other words, what he writes proceeds from a *corrected* banality.

Opacité et transparence ~ Opacity and transparence

Principle of explanation: this work proceeds between two terms:

—at the original term, there is the opacity of social relations. This opacity was immediately exposed in the oppressive form of the stereotype (the obligatory figures of high-school writing, the Communist novels discussed in *Writing Degree Zero*). Subsequently a thousand other forms of the *Doxa;*

—at the final (utopian) term, there is transparence: tender feeling, the vow, the sigh, the desire for rest, as if the consistency of social interlocution might one day be clarified, lightened, aerated to the point of invisibility.

1. The social division produces an opacity (obvious paradox: where there is an extreme of social division, the situation seems opaque, massive).

2. Against this opacity, the subject reacts, opposing it in whatever way he can.

3. However, if he is himself a subject of language, his combat cannot have a direct political outcome, for this would be to return to the opacity of the stereotypes. Hence this combat assumes the movement of an apocalypse: he participates to the utmost, he exasperates a whole set of values, and at the same time he lives utopianly—it might be said he *breathes*—the final transparence of social relations.

L'antithèse ~ Antithesis

Being the figure of opposition, the exasperated form of binarism, Antithesis is the very spectacle of meaning. One emerges from it: either by the neutral, or by the glimpse of reality (the Racinian confidant seeks to abolish the tragic antithesis, as remarked in *On Racine*), or by supplemental material (Balzac supplements the Sarrasinian Antithesis, as remarked in *S/Z*), or by the invention of a third term.

He himself, however, prefers to resort to the Antithesis (for example: "Freedom in the shop window, by virtue of decoration, but order at home, by virtue of constitution," *Mythologies*). Another contradiction? —Yes, and one which will always receive the same explanation: Antithesis is *a theft of language:* I borrow the violence of current discourse for the sake of my own violence, of *meaning-for-myself.*

La défection des origines ~ The abandonment of origins

His work is not anti-historical (at least, so he intends), but always, persistently, antigenetic, for Origin is a pernicious figure of Nature (of Physis): by an abusive interest, the *Doxa* "crushes" Origin and Truth together, in order to make them into a single proof, each reinflating the other, according to a convenient swivel: are not the human sciences *etymological,* in pursuit of the *etymon* (origin and truth) of each phenomenon?

In order to thwart Origin, he first acculturates Nature thoroughly: nothing natural anywhere, nothing but the historical; then this culture (convinced as he is, with Benveniste, that all culture is only language) is restored to the infinite movement of various discourses, set up one against the other (and not engendered) as in hand-over-hand choosing.

Oscillation de la valeur ~ Oscillation of value

On the one hand, Value prevails, determines, separates good from bad (*"neuf"*/*"nouveau,"* structure/structuration, etc.): the world signifies in the strong sense, since everything is caught up in the paradigm of taste and distaste.

On the other hand, every opposition is suspect, meaning exhausts, he wants a rest from it. Value, which armed everything, is disarmed, absorbed into a utopia: no more oppositions, no more meanings, no more Value itself, and this abolition leaves nothing over.

Value (and with it, meaning) thus unceasingly oscillates. The work, in its entirety, limps between an appearance of Manichaeism (when meaning is strong) and an appearance of Pyrrhonism (when its exemption is desired).

Paradoxa ~ Paradoxa

(Correction of Paradox.)

An intense fractionism prevails in the intellectual field: we form oppositions, term for term, as closely as possible, but we remain in the same "repertoire": in animal neuropsychology, the repertoire is the total of impulses according to which the animal functions: why ask the rat a man's questions, since its "repertoire" is that of a rat? Why ask an avant-garde painter a professor's questions? Whereas paradoxal practice develops in a slightly different repertorie, actually that of the writer: we do not form oppositions of *named,* fractionized values; we skirt, we avoid, we dodge such values: *we take tangents;* strictly speaking, this is not a change of course; the fear is that we fall into opposition, aggression, i.e., into meaning (since meaning is never anything but the trip lever of a counter-term, i.e., again: into that semantic solidarity which unites simple contraries.

Le léger moteur de la paranoïa
~ The delicate motor of paranoia

Discreet—ultra-discreet, the motor of paranoia: when he writes (perhaps they all write this way), he keeps his distance as he goes about attacking someone or something unnamed (which he alone can name). What *vindicative* motion has there been at the origin of such a sentence—however general, however dampened? There is no writing which is not, here and there, *underhand.* The motive is erased, the effect subsists: this subtraction defines aesthetic discourse.

Parler / embrasser ~ To speak / to embrace

According to the Leroi-Gourhan hypothesis, it was when he

could free his upper limbs from the task of locomotion and, in consequence, his mouth from predation, that man could speak. I would add: *and embrace*. For the phonatory system is also the osculatory system. Shifting to upright posture, man found himself free to invent language and love: this is perhaps the anthropological birth of a concomitant double perversion: speech and kissing. By this accounting, the freer men have been (with their mouths), the more they have spoken and embraced; and logically, when progress will have rid men of every manual task, they will then do nothing but discourse and make love!

Let us imagine for this double function, localized in one and the same site, a single transgression, which would be generated by a simultaneous use of speech and kissing: *to kiss while embracing, to embrace while speaking*. It would appear that such a pleasure exists, since lovers incessantly "drink in speech upon the lips of the beloved," etc. What they then delight in is, in the erotic encounter, that play of meaning which opens and breaks off: the function *which is disturbed:* in a word: *the stammered body*.

Les corps qui passent ∼ Passing bodies

"One evening, half asleep on a banquette in a bar . . ." (*The Pleasure of the Text*). So that is what I was doing in that Tangier *"boîte"*: I was taking a little nap. Now the *"boîte,"* in the minor sociology of cities, is supposed to be the site of vigilance and action (a matter of speaking, communicating, meeting, etc.); on the contrary, here it is a site of semi-absence. This space is not without bodies—indeed they are quite close by, and this is what is important; but these anonymous bodies, animated by slight movements, leave me in a state of idleness, irresponsibility, and suspension: everyone is here, no one wants anything of me, I gain on both counts: in the *"boîte"* the bodies of others are never transformed into a (civil, psychological, social) "person": they offer me their display, not their interlocution. Like a drug especially adapted to my organism, the *"boîte"* can then become the workshop of my sentences: I do not dream, I make phrases: it is the beheld body and no longer the heard body which assumes a *phatic* function (of contact), now, between the production of my language and the suspended desire on which that production feeds, a relation of vigilance, not of message. The *"boîte"* is in fact a *neutral* place: the utopia of the third term, the drift far from the all-too-pure pair: *speaking/keeping silent.*

On trains, I have ideas: people are moving around me, and the passing bodies act as catalysts. On planes, it is just the contrary: I am motionless, stuck, blind; my body and consequently my intellect are dead: the only thing at my disposal is the movement of the varnished and absent body of the stewardess, circulating like an indifferent mother among the cradles of a day nursery.

Le jeu, le pastiche ~ Play, parody

Among the many illusions he sustains about himself, there is this very tenacious one: that he likes *to play,* and therefore that he has the power to do so; yet he never wrote a parody in his life (at least, of his own free will), except when he was a student in the lycée (of Plato's *Crito*), though he often wanted to. There might be a theoretical reason for this: if it is a question of baffling (*déjouer*) the subject, then playing (*jouer*) is an illusory method, and even contrary in effect to what it seeks to accomplish: the subject of such play is more stable than ever; the real game is not to mask the subject but to mask the playing itself.

Patch-work ~ Patchwork

Self-commentary? What a bore! I had no other solution than to *rewrite* myself—at a distance, a great distance—here and now: to add to the books, to the themes, to the memories, to the texts, another utterance, without my ever knowing whether it is about my past or my present that I am speaking. Whereby I cast over the written work, over the past body and the past corpus, barely brushing against it, a kind of patchwork, a rhapsodic quilt consisting of stitched squares. Far from reaching the core of the matter, I remain on the surface, for this time it is a matter of "myself" (of the Ego); reaching the core, depth, profundity, belongs to others.

La couleur ~ Color

Current opinion always holds sexuality to be aggressive. Hence the notion of a happy, gentle, sensual, jubilant sexuality is never to be found in any text. Where are we to read it, then? In painting, or better still: in color. If I were a painter, I should paint only colors: this field seems to me freed of both the Law (no Imitation, no Analogy) and Nature (for after all, do not all the colors in Nature come from the painters?).

La personne divisée? ~ The person divided?

For classical metaphysics, there was no disadvantage in "dividing" the person (Racine: *J'ai deux hommes en moi*); quite the contrary, decked out in two opposing terms, the person advanced like a good paradigm (*high/low, flesh/spirit, heaven/earth*); the parties to the conflict were reconciled in the establishment of a meaning: the meaning of Man. This is why, when we speak today of a divided subject, it is never to acknowledge his simple contradictions, his double postulations, etc.; it is a *diffraction* which is intended, a dispersion of energy in which there remains neither a central core nor a structure of meaning: I am not contradictory, I am dispersed.

How do you explain, how do you tolerate such contradictions? Philosophically, it seems that you are a materialist (if the word doesn't sound too old-fashioned); ethically, you divide yourself: as for the body, you are a hedonist; as for violence, you would rather be something of a Buddhist! You want to have nothing to do with faith, yet you have a certain nostalgia for ritual, etc. You are a patchwork of reactions: is there anything *primary* in you?

Any classification you read provokes a desire in you to put yourself into it somewhere: where is your place? At first you think you have found it; but gradually, like a disintegrating statue or an eroding relief, its shape blurs and fades, or better still, like Harpo Marx losing his artificial beard in the glass of water he is drinking out of, you are no longer classifiable, not out of an excess of personality, but on the contrary because you pass through all the fringes of the phantom, the specter: you unite in yourself supposedly distinctive features which henceforth no longer distinguish anything; you discover that you are at one and the same time (or alternately) obsessive, hysterical, paranoiac, and perverse to the last degree (not to mention certain erotic psychoses), or that you sum up all the decadent philosophies: Epicureanism, eudaemonism, Asianism, Manichaeism, Pyrrhonism.

"Everything has happened in us because we are ourselves, always ourselves, and never one minute the same" (Diderot, *Réfutation d'Helvétius*).

Partitif ~ Partitive

Petit bourgeois: this predicate can be fastened to any subject; no one is safe from this evil (naturally enough: all of French culture, far beyond the books, is subject to it): in the worker, in the executive, in the professor, in the student protest leader, in the militant, in my friends X, Y, and in me, of course, *there is something petit bourgeois:* a massive-partitive. Now, there is another object of language which affords the same mobile and panic character: the Text: I cannot say that this or that work is a Text, but only that within it *there is something of the Text. Text* and *petit bourgeois* thereby form one and the same universal substance, on the one hand noxious, on the other exciting; they have the same discursive function: that of a universal operator of value.

Bataille, la peur ~ Bataille, fear

Bataille, after all, affects me little enough: what have I to do with laughter, devotion, poetry, violence? What have I to say about "the sacred," about "the impossible"?

Yet no sooner do I make all this (alien) language coincide with that disturbance in myself which I call *fear* than Bataille conquers me all over again: then everything he *inscribes describes* me: it sticks.

Intertext	Genre	Works
(Gide)	(desire to write)	–
Sartre Marx Brecht	social mythology	*Writing Degree Zero* Writings on theater *Mythologies*
Saussure	semiology	*Elements of Semiology* *Système de la mode*
Sollers, Kristeva Derrida, Lacan	textuality	*S/Z* *Sade, Fourier, Loyola* *L'Empire des signes*
(Nietzsche)	morality	*The Pleasure of the Text* *Roland Barthes by Roland Barthes*

Remarks: (1) The intertext is not necessarily a field of influences; rather it is a music of figures, metaphors, thought-words; it is the signifier as *siren;* (2) *morality* should be understood as the precise opposite of ethics (it is the thinking of the body in a state of language); (3) first of all (mythological) *interventions,* then (semiological) *fictions,* then splinters, fragments, *sentences, phrases;* (4) between the periods, obviously, there are overlappings, returns, affinities, leftovers; it is usually the (magazine) articles which are responsible for this conjunctive role; (5) each phase is reactive: the author reacts either to the discourse which surrounds him, or to his own discourse, if one and the other begin to have too much consistency, too much stability; (6) as one nail drives out another, so they say, a perversion drives out a neurosis: political and moral obsession is followed by a minor scientific delirium, which in its turn sets off a perverse pleasure (with its undercurrent of fetishism); (7) the articulation of a period, of a work, into phases of development—though this be a matter of an imaginary operation—permits entering the interaction of intellectual communication: one makes oneself *intelligible.*

Structuralist fashions

Fashion affects the body. By fashion, I return in my text as farce, as caricature. A kind of collective "id" replaces the image I thought I had of myself, and that "id" is me

Effet bienfaisant d'une phrase ~ Beneficent effect of a phrase

X tells me that one day he decided "to exonerate his life from his unhappy loves," and that this *phrase* seemed so splendid to him that it almost managed to compensate for the failures which had provoked it; he then determined (and determined me) to take more advantage of this *reservoir of irony* in all (aesthetic) language.

Le texte politique ~ The political text

The Political is, subjectively, a continuous source of boredom and/or pleasure; it is, further and *in fact* (i.e., despite the arrogances of the political subject), a stubbornly polysemant space, the privileged site of a perpetual interpretation (if it is sufficiently systematic, an interpretation will never be contradicted here, to infinity). One might conclude from these two observations that the Political partakes of the pure *textual:* an exorbitant, exasperated form of the Text, an unheard-of form which, by its excesses and its masks, perhaps exceeds our present understanding of the Text. And Sade having produced the purest of texts, I believe I understand that the Political pleases me as a *Sadean* text and displeases me as a *Sadistic* text.

L'alphabet ~ The alphabet

Temptation of the alphabet: to adopt the succession of letters in order to link fragments is to fall back on what constitutes the glory of language (and what constituted Saussure's despair): an unmotivated order (an order outside of any imitation), which is not arbitrary (since everyone knows it, recognizes it, and agrees on it). The alphabet is euphoric: no more anguish of "schema," no more rhetoric of "development," no more twisted logic, no more dissertations! an idea per fragment, a fragment per idea, and as for the succession of these atoms, nothing but the age-old and irrational order of the French letters (which are themselves meaningless objects—deprived of meaning).

It does not define a word, it names a fragment; it does precisely the converse of a dictionary: the word emerges from the utterance, rather than the utterance proceeding from the word. Of the glossary, I keep only its most formal principle: the order of its units. This order, however, can be mischievous: it sometimes produces effects of meaning; and if these effects are not desired, the alphabet must be broken up to the advantage of a superior rule: that of the breach (heterology): to keep a meaning from "taking."

L'ordre dont je ne me souviens plus
~ The order I no longer remember

He more or less remembers the order in which he wrote these fragments; but where did that order come from? In the course of what classification, of what succession? He no longer remembers. The alphabetical order erases everything, banishes every origin. Perhaps in places, certain fragments seem to follow one another by some affinity; but the important thing is that these little networks not be connected, that they not slide into a single enormous network which would be the structure of the book, its meaning. It is in order to halt, to deflect, to divide this descent of discourse toward a destiny of the subject, that at certain moments the alphabet calls you to order (to disorder) and says: *Cut! Resume the story in another way* (but also, sometimes, for the same reason, you must break up the alphabet).

L'oeuvre comme polygraphie ~ The work as polygraphy

I can imagine an antistructural criticism; it would not look for the work's order but its disorder; for this it would suffice to consider any work as an *encyclopedia:* cannot each text be defined by the number of disparate objects (of knowledge, of sensuality) which it brings into view with the help of simple figures of contiguity (metonymies and asyndetons)? Like the encyclopedia, the work exhausts a list of heterogeneous objects, and this list is the work's antistructure, its obscure and irrational polygraphy.

Le langage-prêtre ～ Language-as-priest

With regard to ritual, is it so disagreeable to be a priest? As for faith, what human subject can predict that he will not someday conform to his own economy of "belief"—in this or in that? It is with regard to language that this would not work: language-as-priest? Impossible.

Le discours prévisible ～ Foreseeable discourse

Tedium of foreseeable discourse. Foreseeability is a structural category, since it is possible to give the modes of expectation or of encounter (in short: of *suspense*) of which language is the theater (this has been done for narrative); we might then establish a typology of the various kinds of discourse according to their degree of foreseeability. *Text of the Dead:* a litaneutical text, in which no word can be changed.

(Last evening, after writing this: in the restaurant, at the very next table, two individuals were talking, not very loud, but in very clear, well-pitched, nicely trained voices, as if a school of diction had prepared them to be overheard by their neighbors in public places: everything they said, sentence by sentence [about several first names of their friends, about Pasolini's latest film], everything is entirely in accordance, foreseen: no flaw in the endoxal system. Agreement between this voice, which chooses no one, and the inexorable *Doxa:* this is *jactancy,* boasting.)

Projets de livres ～ Projected books

(These ideas are from different periods): *Journal of Desire* (Desire's daily entries, in the field of reality). *The Sentence* (ideology and erotics of the Sentence). *Our France* (new mythologies of today's France; or rather: am I happy/unhappy to be French?). *The Amateur* (record what happens to me when I paint). *Linguistics of Intimidation* (of Value, of the war of meanings). *A Thousand Fantasies* (to write one's fantasies, not one's dreams). *Ethology of the*

Intellectuals (quite as important as the behavior of ants). *The Discourse of Homosexuality* (or: the discourses of homosexuality, or again: the discourse of homosexualities). An *Encyclopedia of Food* (dietetics, history, economy, geography, and above all, *symbolics*). A *Life of Illustrious Men* (read a lot of biographies and collect certain features, biographemes, as was done for Sade and Fourier). A *Compilation of Visual Stereotypes* ("Saw a North African in dark clothes, *Le Monde* under his arm, paying court to a blond girl sitting in a café"). *The Book/Life* (take some classic book and relate everything in life to it for a year). *Incidents* (mini-texts, one-liners, haiku, notations, puns, everything that falls, like a leaf), etc.

Rapport à la psychanalyse ~ Relation to psychoanalysis

His relation to psychoanalysis is not scrupulous (though without his being able to pride himself on any contestation, any rejection). It is an *undecided* relation.

Psychanalyse et psychologie ~ Psychoanalysis and psychology

For psychoanalysis to be able to speak, it must be able to appropriate a different discourse—a slightly clumsy discourse, which is not yet psychoanalytic. This distant discourse, this *retarded* discourse—burdened by old culture and rhetoric—this is, in patches, psychological discourse. In short, it would be the function of psychology to offer itself as a good object to psychoanalysis.

(Truckling to what has an advantage over you; for example, at the Lycée Louis-le-Grand, I had a history professor who, requiring to be jeered as though it were a daily drug, stubbornly offered the students a thousand opportunities for making a racket: howlers, naïvetés, double entendres, ambiguous gestures, and even the melancholy with which he accompanied all this secretly provocative behavior; the students, having quickly realized this, abstained, on certain days, quite sadistically, from jeering him.)

"Qu'est-ce que ça veut dire?" ~ "What does that mean?"

Constant (and illusory) passion for applying to every phenomenon, even the merest, not the child's question: *Why?* but the ancient Greek's question, the question of meaning, as if all things shuddered with meaning: *What does that mean?* The fact must be transformed at all costs into idea, into description, into interpretation, in short, there must be found for it *a name other than its own.* This mania is no respecter of futility: for instance, if I observe— and I am eager to observe it—that in the country I enjoy pissing in the garden and not anywhere else, I immediately want to know *what that signifies.* This rage to make the simplest facts signify marks the subject, socially, like a voice: *the chain of names must not be broken, language must not be unchained:* excess of nomination is always held up to ridicule (M. Jourdain, Bouvard and Pécuchet).

(Even here, except in the *Anamneses,* whose value is precisely in this fact, nothing is reported without making it signify; one dares not leave the fact in a state of in-significance; this is the movement of fable, which draws from each fragment of reality a lesson, a meaning. A converse book is conceivable: which would report a thousand "incidents" but would refuse ever to draw a line of meaning from them; this would be, quite specifically, a book of haiku.)

Quel raisonnement? ~ Which reasoning?

Japan is a positive value, prattle a negative value. Now the Japanese prattle. This need be no obstacle: it will suffice to say that this particular prattle is not negative ("It is the whole body . . . which enters with you into a kind of prattle from which the perfect domination of the codes strips any regressive, infantile character," *L'Empire des signes*). R.B. does exactly what he says Michelet does: "There does exist a certain type of Micheletist causality, but such causality remains cautiously relegated to the improbable regions of morality. These are certain 'necessities' of a moral order, entirely psychological postulates . . . : Greece *must not* have been homosexual, since Greece is all light, etc" (*Michelet*). The Japanese prattle *must not* be regressive, since the Japanese are lovable.

The "reasoning" consists, in short, of a series of metaphors: he takes a phenomenon (connotation, the letter Z) and he submits it to an avalanche of points of view; what replaces argumentation is the unfolding of an image: Michelet "eats" History; hence he "grazes" on it; hence he "walks" in it, etc.: everything that happens to an animal put out to pasture will thus be *applied* to Michelet: the metaphoric application will play the part of an explanation.

One might call "poetic" (without value judgment) any discourse in which the word leads the idea: if you like words to the point of succumbing to them, you exclude yourself from the law of the signified, from *écrivance*. This is an *oneiric* discourse to the letter (our dreams seize the words which pass under their nose and make them into a story). My body itself (and not only my ideas) can *make up to* words, can be in some sense created by them: today, I discover on my tongue a red patch which appears to be an abrasion, or in medical terms an excoriation—painless, moreover, which fits in perfectly, I decide, with cancer! But examined closely, this sign is merely a faint desquamation of the whitish film which covers the tongue. I cannot swear that this whole little obsessive scenario has not been worked up in order to use that rare word, so attractive by dint of its exactitude: *excoriation*.

La récession ~ Recession

In all this there are risks of recession: the subject speaks about himself (risk of psychologism, risk of infatuation), he offers his discourse in fragments (risk of aphorism, risk of arrogance).

This book consists of what I do not know: the unconscious and ideology, things which utter themselves only by the voices of others. I cannot put on stage (in the text), *as such,* the symbolic and the ideological which pass through me, since I am their blind spot (what actually belongs to me is *my* image-repertoire, my phantasmatics: whence this book). I can make use of psychoanalysis and of political criticism, then, only in the fashion of Orpheus: without ever turning around, without ever looking at them, declaring them (or so little: just enough to restore my interpretation to the course of the image-system).

The title of this series of books (*X by himself*) has an analytic bearing: *myself by myself?* But that is the very program of the image-system! How is it that the rays of the mirror reverberate on me? Beyond that zone of diffraction—the only one upon which I can cast a glance, though without ever being able to exclude from it the very one who will speak about it—there is reality, and there is also the symbolic. For the latter, I have no responsibility (I have quite enough to do, dealing with my own image-repertoire!): to the Other, to the transference, and hence *to the reader*.

And all this happens, as is obvious here, through the Mother, present next to the Mirror.

Le réflexe structural ~ The structural reflex

Just as the athlete delights in his good reflexes, the semiologist likes to be able to grasp readily the functioning of a paradigm. Reading Freud's *Moses and Monotheism,* he enjoys catching the pure triggering of meaning; his enjoyment is all the stronger in that here it is the opposition of two simple letters which step by step leads to the opposition of two religions: *Amon/Aton:* the whole history of Judaism in the shift from ''m'' to ''t.''

(The structural reflex consists in deferring the pure difference as long as possible to the end of a common stem: so that the meaning explode, pure and clear, *in extremis;* so that the victory of meaning be won in the nick of time, as in a good thriller.)

Le règne et le triomphe ~ Reign and triumph

In the pandemonium of social discourse, of the great sociolects, let us distinguish two kinds of arrogance, two monstrous modes of rhetorical domination: *Reign* and *Triumph.* The *Doxa* is not triumphalist; it is content to reign; it diffuses, blurs; it is a legal, a natural dominance; a general layer, spread with the blessing of Power; a universal Discourse, a mode of jactancy which is already lurking in the mere fact of "holding" a discourse (upon something): whence the natural affinity between endoxal discourse and radiophony: upon Pompidou's death, for three days, *it flowed, it broadcast.* Quite the contrary, militant language, whether revolutionary or religious (in the days when religion militated), is a triumphant language: each action of the discourse is a triumph *à l'antique:* the victors and the defeated enemies are made to parade past. One could measure the mode of assurance of political systems and detail their development depending on whether they are (still) in Triumph or (already) in Reign. One would have to study, for example, how—at what rhythm, according to what figures—the Revolutionary triumphalism of 1793 was gradually tamed, diffused, how it "took," shifting to the state of Reign (of bourgeois language).

Abolition du règne des valeurs
~ Abolition of the reign of values

Contradiction: a whole long text on value, on a continuous affect of evaluation—which involves an activity at once ethical and semantic—and at the same time, *and precisely because of that,* an equal energy in dreaming of an "abolition without leftovers of the reign of values" (which was, it is said, the purpose of Zen).

Qu'est-ce qui limite la représentation?
~ What limits representation?

Brecht had wet laundry put in the actress's laundry basket so that her hip would have the right movement, that of the alienated laundress. Well and good; but stupid too, no? For what weighs down the basket is not wet laundry but time, history, and how *represent* such a weight as that? It is impossible to represent the political: it resists all copying, even when you turn yourself out to give it all the more verisimilitude. Contrary to the inveterate belief of all socialist arts, where politics begins is where imitation ceases.

COMPOSITION FRANÇAISE *

Durée : 6 heures

___

« Le style est presque au-delà [de la Littérature] : des images, un débit, un lexique naissent du corps et du passé de l'écrivain et deviennent peu à peu les automatismes mêmes de son art. Ainsi sous le nom de style, se forme un langage autarcique qui ne plonge que dans la mythologie personnelle et secrète de l'auteur... où se forme le premier couple des mots et des choses, où s'installent une fois pour toutes les grands thèmes verbaux de son existence. Quel que soit son raffinement, le style a toujours quelque chose de brut : il est une forme sans destination, il est le produit d'une poussée, non d'une intention, il est comme une dimension verticale et solitaire de la pensée. [...] Le style est proprement un phénomène d'ordre germinatif, il est la transmutation d'une humeur. [...] Le miracle de cette transmutation fait du style une sorte d'opération supralittéraire, qui emporte l'homme au seuil de la puissance et de la magie. Par son origine biologique, le style se situe hors de l'art, c'est-à-dire hors du pacte qui lie l'écrivain à la société. On peut donc imaginer des auteurs qui préfèrent la sécurité de l'art à la solitude du style. »

R. BARTHES, *Le degré zéro de l'écriture,* chap. I.

Par une analyse de ce texte, vous dégagerez la conception du style que propose R. Barthes et vous l'apprécierez en vous référant à des exemples littéraires.

* Rapport de Mme Châtelet

Les candidates ont été placées cette année devant un texte long de Roland BARTHES. On leur demandait : - d'abord de l'analyser pour en dégager les idées de Roland Barthes sur le style,

- puis d'apprécier librement cette conception.

Un grand nombre d'entre elles ayant paru déroutées par l'analyse, nous insisterons sur cet exercice. Nous indiquerons ensuite les principales directions dans lesquelles pouvait s'engager la discussion.

I - L'ANALYSE

L'analyse suppose d'abord une lecture attentive du passage proposé. Or beaucoup de copies révèlent des faiblesses sur ce point. Rappelons donc quelques règles essentielles sur la manière de lire un texte.

Puisqu'il ne peut s'agir ici d'une lecture expressive à voix haute, on conseillerait volontiers une lecture annotée, qui n'hésite pas à souligner les mots importants, les liaisons indispensables, qui mette en évidence les parallélismes ou les reprises d'expression, bref qui dégage par des moyens matériels la structure du texte. Cette première lecture n'a pour objet que de préparer l'analyse qui doit être elle-même élaborée à partir des éléments retenus.

Récupération.

Le retentissement ~ Repercussion

Every word which concerns him echoes within him to an extreme degree, and it is this repercussion which he dreads, to the point of timidly avoiding any discourse that might be offered about him. The language of others, complimentary or not, is tainted at its source by the repercussion it might have. Only he, because he knows its point of departure, can measure the effort necessary for him to read a text if it discusses himself. The link to the world is thus always conquered starting from a certain fear.

Réussi / raté ~ Success / failure

Rereading himself, he discerns in the very texture of each piece of writing a singular cleavage: that of *success/failure:* in gusts, felicities of expression, good patches, then bad ones, swamps and deserts which he has even begun to inventory. Then no book is successful throughout? —Probably the book on Japan. A happy sexuality doubtless finds its corresponding discourse quite naturally in the continuous, effusive, jubilant happiness of the writing: *in what he writes, each protects his own sexuality.*

A third category is possible: neither success nor failure: disgrace: marked, branded with the imaginary.

Du choix d'un vêtement ~ Choosing clothes

A TV film on Rosa Luxemburg shows me the beauty of her face. From her eyes, I conceive a desire to read her books. Whereupon I conceive a fiction: that of an intellectual subject who decides to become a Marxist and who must choose his Marxism: which one? of what provenance, what brand? Lenin, Trotsky, Luxemburg, Bakunin, Mao, Bordiga, etc.? This subject walks into a library, reads everything, the way one handles the clothes in a store, and selects the Marxism which suits him best, preparing himself to sustain henceforth the discourse of truth starting from an economy which is that of his own body.

(This could be an unpublished scene from *Bouvard and Pécu-*

chet—if it were not for the fact that Bouvard and Pécuchet
changed bodies in each library they explored.)

Le rhythme ~ Rhythm

He has always put his faith in that Greek rhythm, the succession of *Ascesis* and Festivity, the release of one by the other (and
not the banal rhythm of modernity: *work/leisure*). This was Michelet's rhythm, in life as in texts passing through a cycle of deaths
and resurrections, migraines and high spirits, narratives (he "la-
bored" through Louis XI) and scenes (where his writing blos-
somed). This was the rhythm he experienced something of in Ru-
mania, where, by a Slavic or Balkan custom, one periodically *shut
oneself up* for three days in Festivity (games, food, sleepless
nights, etc.: this was "kef"). And in his own life he keeps seeking
this rhythm; not only the fact that during the workday he must *have
in view* the night's pleasure (which is banal enough), but also, com-
plementarily, that out of the happy evening dawns, at its end, the
craving to be already back at work (writing) and on with the next
morning.

(Note that this rhythm is not necessarily a regular one: Casals
once remarked very appropriately that rhythm is all in the *retard*.)

Que ça se sache ~ Let that be known

Every utterance of a writer (even the fiercest, the wildest)
includes a secret operator, an unexpressed word, something like the
silent morpheme of a category as primitive as negation or interroga-
tion, whose meaning is: *"And let that be known!"* This message
stamps the sentences of any writing; in each of them there is a tone,
a sound, a muscular, laryngeal tension which reminds me of the
three knocks at the theater or of Rank's gong. Even Artaud, the
heterological god, says of what he writes: *Let that be known!*

Entre Salamanque et Valladolid
~ Between Salamanca and Valladolid

One summer day (1970) driving and daydreaming between Salamanca and Valladolid, he diverted himself by imagining a kind of new philosophy which he forthwith baptized "preferentialism," heedless, there in his car, whether it was frivolous or guilty: against a materialist background (a cliff?) in which the world is seen as no more than a fabric, a text unrolling the revolution of languages, the war of systems, and in which the subject—scattered, deconstructed—can grasp himself only by means of an image-repertoire, the (political, ethical) choice of this apparent subject has no establishing value: *such a choice is not important;* whatever the style—pompous or violent—in which it is declared, it is never anything but an *inclination:* in the presence of the world's *fragments,* I am entitled only to *preference.*

Exercice scolaire ~ Academic exercise

1. Why does the author mention the date of this episode?
2. How does the site justify "daydreaming" and "diversion"?
3. How might the philosophy the author describes be "guilty"?
4. Explain the metaphor "fabric."
5. Cite the philosophies to which "preferentialism" might be opposed.
6. Meanings of the words "revolution," "system," "image-repertoire," "inclination."
7. Why does the author put certain words or expressions in italics?
8. Characterize the author's style.

Le savoir et l'écriture ~ Scholarship and writing

Working on some text which is well under way, he likes to look up details, corroborations, in works of scholarship; if he could, he would have an exemplary library of reference works (dictionaries, encyclopedias, manuals, etc.): so that scholarship would be in a circle around me, at my disposal; so that I need merely *consult* it—and not ingest it; so that scholarship be kept in its place as a *complement of writing*.

Le valeur et le savoir ~ Value and scholarship

Apropos of Bataille: "In short, scholarship is reserved as potentiality, but it is opposed as boredom; value is not what scorns, relativizes, or rejects scholarship, but what exorcises it of boredom, what *spells* it from boredom; value does not confront scholarship in a polemical perspective but in a structural sense; there is an alternation of scholarship and value, a *spelling* of one by the other, according to a kind of *amorous rhythm*. And this is what constitutes the writing of Bataille's essays: the amorous rhythm of science and of value: heterology, bliss.''

La scène ~ Scenes

He has always regarded the (domestic) "scene" as a pure experience of violence, to the degree that, wherever he encounters it, the scene always inspires *fear,* as though he were a child panic-stricken by his parents' quarrels (he always avoids scenes, shamelessly). If scenes have such a repercussion for him, it is because they lay bare the cancer of language. Language is impotent to close language—that is what the scene says: the retorts engender one another, without any possible conclusion, save that of murder; and it is because the scene is entirely bent on, aims toward this ultimate violence, which nonetheless it never assumes (at least among "civilized" people), that it is an essential violence, a violence which delights in sustaining itself: terrible and ridiculous, like some sort of science-fiction homeostat.

(On stage, the scene is domesticated: the theater *humbles* it, obliges it to end: a cessation of language is the greatest violence that can be done to the violence of language.)

159

He had a low threshold of tolerance for violence. This disposition, though constantly verified, remained quite enigmatic to him; but he felt that the reason for this intolerance was to be found in this direction: violence always organized itself into a *scene:* the most transitive of behavior (to eliminate, to kill, to wound, to humble) was also the most theatrical, and it was really this kind of semantic scandal he so resisted (is not meaning by its very nature opposed to action?); in all violence, he could not keep from discerning, strangely, a literary kernel: how many conjugal scenes must be classified under the label of some great genre painting: *the wife cast out* or, again, *the repudiation!* In short, all violence is the illustration of a pathetic stereotype, and strangely, it was the quite non-realistic way in which the violent action is embellished and encumbered—a grotesque and expeditious fashion, at once active and paralyzed—which made violence awaken in him a sentiment he experienced on no other occasion: a kind of severity (no doubt the stock reaction of an intellectual, of a "clerk").

La science dramatisée ~ Science dramatized

He suspected Science, reproaching it for what Nietzsche calls its *adiaphoria,* its in-difference, erected into a Law by the scientists who constituted themselves its procurators. Yet his condemnation dissolved each time it was possible to *dramatize* Science (to restore to it a power of difference, a textual effect); he liked the scientists in whom he could discern a disturbance, a vacillation, a mania, a delirium, an inflection; he had learned a great deal from Saussure's *Cours,* but Saussure had come to mean infinitely more to him since he discovered the man's desperate pursuit of the Anagrams; in many scientists, he suspected a similar kind of happy flaw, but for the most part, they dared not proceed to the point of making a whole work out of such a thing: their utterance remained choked, stiff, indifferent.

Thus, he thought, it was because it could not be *carried away* that semiological science had not turned out well: it was so often no more than a murmur of indifferent labors, each of which made no differentiation among object, text, body. Yet how could it be forgotten that semiology has some relation to the passion of meaning: its apocalypse and/or its utopia?

The *corpus:* what a splendid idea! Provided one was willing to read *the body* in the corpus: either because in the group of texts reserved for study (and which form the corpus) the pursuit is no longer of structure alone but of the figures of the utterance; or because one has a certain erotic relation with this group of texts (without which the corpus is merely a scientific *image-repertoire*).

Always remember Nietzsche: we are scientific out of a lack of subtlety. —I can conceive, on the contrary, as a kind of utopia, a dramatic and subtle science, seeking the festive reversal of the Aristotelian proposition and which would dare to think, at least in a flash: *There is no science except of differences*.

Je vois le langage ~ I see language

I have a disease: I *see* language. What I should simply hear, a strange pulsion—perverse in that in it desire mistakes its object, reveals it to me as a "vision," analogous (all allowances made) to the one Scipio had in his dream of the musical spheres of the world. The primal scene, in which I listen without seeing, is followed by a perverse scene, in which I imagine seeing what I am hearing. Hearing deviates to scopia: I feel myself to be the visionary and voyeur of language.

According to an initial vision, the image-repertoire is simple: it is the discourse of others *insofar as I see it* (I put it between quotation marks). Then I turn the scopia on myself: I see my language *in so far as it is seen:* I see it *naked* (without quotation marks): this is the disgraced, pained phase of the image-repertoire. A third vision then appears: that of infinitely spread-out languages, of parentheses never to be closed: a utopian vision in that it supposes a mobile, plural reader, who nimbly inserts and removes the quotation marks: who begins to write *with me*.

Sed contra ~ Sed contra

Frequently he starts from the stereotype, from the banal opinion *which is in him.* And it is because he does not want that stereotype (by some aesthetic or individualist reflex) that he looks for something else; habitually, being soon wearied, he halts at the mere contrary opinion, at paradox, at what mechanically denies the prejudice (for example: "there is no science except of the particular"). He sustains, in short, counter-relations with the stereotype—familial relations.

It is a kind of intellectual "sport": he systematically goes where there is a solidification of language, a consistency, a stereotypy. Like a watchful cook, he makes sure that language does not thicken, that it doesn't *stick.* This movement, one of pure form, accounts for the progressions and regressions of the work: it is a pure language tactic, which is deployed *in the air,* without any strategic horizon. The risk is that since the stereotype shifts historically, politically, it must be followed wherever it goes: what is to be done if the stereotype *goes left?*

La seiche et son encre ~ The cuttlefish and its ink

I am writing this day after day; it takes, it sets: the cuttlefish produces its ink: I tie up my image-system (in order to protect myself and at the same time to offer myself).

How will I know that the book is finished? In other words, as always, it is a matter of elaborating a language. Now, in every language the signs return, and by dint of returning they end by saturating the lexicon—the work. Having uttered the substance of these fragments for some months, what happens to me subsequently is arranged quite spontaneously (without forcing) under the utterances that have already been made: the structure is gradually woven, and in creating itself, it increasingly magnetizes: thus it constructs for itself, without any plan on my part, a repertoire which is both finite and perpetual, like that of language. At a certain moment, no further transformation is possible but the one which occurred to the

The adventurous idea.
Still warm, nothing is yet to be
determined of its quality: stupid?
dangerous? insignificant? worth keeping?
to be thrown away? to be focused? to be protected?

ship *Argo:* I could keep the book a very long time, by gradually changing each of its fragments.

Projet d'un livre sur la sexualité
~ A projected book on sexuality

A young couple comes into my compartment and sits down; the woman is blond, made up; she is wearing big dark glasses, reads *Paris-Match;* she has a ring on each finger, and each nail on both hands is painted a different color from its two neighbors; the nail of the middle finger, a shorter nail painted a deep carmine, broadly designates the finger of masturbation. From this—from the *enchantment* this couple casts upon me, so that I cannot take my eyes off them—comes the idea of a book (or of a film) in which there would be, in this way, nothing but secondary sex characteristics (nothing pornographic); in it one would grasp (would try to grasp) the sexual "personality" of each body, which is neither its beauty nor even its "sexiness" but the way in which each sexuality immediately lets itself be read; for the young blonde with the harlequin nails and her young husband with his tight pants and warm eyes were wearing their couple-sexuality like the legion-of-honor ribbon in a buttonhole (*sexuality* and *respectability* relating to the same kind of display), and this *legible* sexuality (as Michelet would certainly have read it) filled the compartment, by an irresistible metonymy, much more certainly than any series of coquetries.

Le sexy ~ Sexiness

Different from secondary sexuality, the sexiness of a body (which is not its beauty) inheres in the fact that it is possible to discern (to fantasize) in it the erotic practice to which one subjects it in thought (I conceive of this particular practice, specifically, and of no other). Similarly, distinguished within the text, one might say that there are *sexy sentences:* disturbing by their very isolation, as if they possessed the promise which is made to us, the readers, by a linguistic practice, as if we were to seek them out by virtue of a pleasure *which knows what it wants.*

Fin heureuse de la sexualité? ~ Sexuality's happy ending?

The Chinese: everyone asks (and I first among them): But where is there sexuality? —A vague notion of this (actually, an imagination), but if it were true, this would be a revulsion from a whole previous discourse: in Antonioni's film, we see people examining in a museum a model representing a barbaric scene of ancient China: a band of soldiers is pillaging a family of poor peasants; the expressions are brutal or suffering; the model is a large one, well lighted, the bodies are at once frozen (in the shimmer of the wax museum) and contorted, wrought to a kind of paroxysm which is both carnal and semantic; one thinks of the realistic sculptures of the Spanish Christs, whose crudity so revolted Renan (it is true that he imputed it to the Jesuits). Now that scene suddenly seems to me, quite specifically, *oversexualized,* in the fashion of a Sadean tableau. And then I imagine (but this is only an imagination) that sexuality, *as we speak it, and insofar as we speak it,* is a product of social oppression, of men's wicked history: an effect of civilization, in other words. Whence it might be that sexuality, *our* sexuality, would be exempted, dismissed, annulled, *without repression,* by social liberation: the Phallus done away with! It is we who, in the manner of the ancient pagans, make it into a little god. Might not materialism pass through a certain sexual *distancing,* the *matte* fall of sexuality outside discourse, outside science?

Le shifter comme utopie ~ The shifter as utopia

He receives a card from a faraway friend: *"Monday. Returning tomorrow. Jean-Louis."*

Like Monsieur Jourdain and his famous prose (moreover, a more or less Poujadist scene), he marvels at discovering in so simple an utterance the trace of those double operators, *shifters,* analyzed by Jakobson. For if Jean-Louis knows perfectly well who he is and on what day he is writing, once his message is in my hands it is entirely uncertain: *which Monday? which Jean-Louis?* How would I be able to tell, since *from my point of view* I must instantly choose between more than one Jean-Louis and several Mondays? Though coded, to speak only of the most familiar of these operators, the shifter thus appears as a complex means—furnished by language itself—of breaking communication: I speak (consider my mastery of the code) but I wrap myself in the mist of an enunciatory situation which is unknown to you; I insert into my discourse certain *leaks of interlocution* (is this not, in fact, what always happens when we utilize that shifter *par excellence,* the pronoun *I?*). Which leads him to imagine shifters (let us call shifters, by extension, all operators of uncertainty formed *at the level of language itself: I, here, now, tomorrow, Monday, Jean-Louis*) as so many social subversions, conceded by language but opposed by society, which fears such leaks of subjectivity and always stops them by insisting on reducing the operator's duplicity (*Monday, Jean-Louis*) by the "objective" memorandum of a date (*Monday, March 12*) or of a patronymic (*Jean-Louis B.*). Can we even imagine the freedom and, so to speak, the erotic fluidity of a collectivity which would speak only in pronouns and shifters, each person never saying anything but *I, tomorrow, over there,* without referring to anything legal whatsoever, and in which the *vagueness of difference* (the only fashion of respecting its subtlety, its infinite repercussion) would be language's most precious value?

Dans la signification, trois choses
~ In signification, three things

In signification, as it has been conceived since the Stoic philosophers, there are three things: the signifier, the signified, and the referent. But now, if I imagine a linguistics of value (yet how construct such a linguistics while oneself remaining outside of value, how construct it "scientifically," "linguistically"?), these three things which are in signification are no longer the same; one is known, which is the process of signification, the ordinary realm of classical linguistics, which stops here, abides here, and forbids us to go further, but the others are less familiar. They are *notification* (I plant my message and I assign my auditor) and *signature* (I display myself, I cannot avoid displaying myself). By this analysis, one would merely unfold the etymology of the verb "signify": to fabricate a sign, to make a sign (to someone), to reduce oneself in terms of the image-system to one's own sign, to sublimate oneself within it.

Une philosophie simpliste ~ A simplistic philosophy

It frequently seems that he regards sociality simplistically: as an enormous and perpetual friction of languages (discourses, fictions, image-systems, reasonings, systems, sciences) and desires (impulses, injuries, resentments, etc.). Then what does "reality" become in such a philosophy? It is not denied (often, in fact, invoked, on progressive claims), but referred, actually, to a kind of "technique," of empirical rationality, the object of "formulae," of "remedies," of "solutions" (*if one does this, one produces that; in order to avoid this, it is only reasonable to do that; here we must wait and let matters transform themselves, etc.*). Philosophy with a maximum gap: raving with respect to language, empirical (and "progressive") with respect to "reality."
(Always this French rejection of Hegelianism.)

Singe entre les singes ~ Monkey among the monkeys

Acosta, a Portuguese gentleman of Jewish stock, is exiled to Amsterdam; he belongs to the synagogue; however, his criticisms of it cause him to be excommunicated by the rabbis; he should then, logically, cut himself off from the Hebrew communion, but he concludes otherwise: "Why should I persist in remaining separate from it all my life with so many disadvantages, since I am in a foreign country where I do not even speak the language? *Would it not be a wiser course to play monkey among the monkeys?*" (Pierre Bayle, *Dictionnaire historique et critique*).
When no known language is available to you, you must determine *to steal a language*—as men used to steal a loaf of bread. (All those—legion—who are outside Power are obliged to steal language.)

167

La division sociale ∼ Social division

The divisions of social relationship certainly exist, they are real, he does not deny it and confidently listens to all those (and they are numerous) who discuss them; but in his eyes, and doubtless because he somewhat fetishizes language, these real divisions are absorbed in their interlocutive form: it is interlocution which is divided, alienated: hence he experiences the entire social relationship in terms of language.

Moi, je ∼ Myself, I

An American (or positivist, or disputatious: I cannot disentangle) student identifies, as if it were self-evident, *subjectivity* and *narcissism;* no doubt he thinks that subjectivity consists in talking about oneself, and in speaking well of oneself. This is because he is a victim of the old couple, the old paradigm: *subjectivity/objectivity.* Yet today the subject apprehends himself *elsewhere,* and "subjectivity" can return at another place on the spiral: deconstructed, taken apart, shifted, without anchorage: why should I not speak of "myself" since this "my" is no longer "the self"?

The so-called personal pronouns: everything happens here, I am forever enclosed within the pronominal lists: "I" mobilize the image-repertoire, "you" and "he" mobilize paranoia. But also, fugitively, according to the reader, everything, like the reflections of a watered silk, can be reversed: in "myself, I," the "I" might not be "me," the "me" he so ostentatiously puts down; I can say to myself "you" as Sade did, in order to detach within myself the worker, the fabricator, the producer of writing, from the subject of the work (the Author); on the other hand, not to speak of oneself can mean: *I am He who does not speak about himself;* and to speak about oneself by saying "he" can mean: *I am speaking about myself as though I were more or less dead,* caught up in a faint mist of paranoiac rhetoric, or again: I am speaking about myself in the manner of the Brechtian actor who must distance his character: "show" rather than incarnate him, and give his manner of speaking a kind of fillip whose effect is to pry the pronoun from its name, the image from its support, the image-repertoire from its mirror (Brecht recommended that the actor think out his entire role in the third person).

Possible affinity of paranoia and distancing, by the intermediary of narrative: the "he" is epic. Which means: "he" is wicked: the nastiest word in the language: pronoun of the non-person, it annuls and mortifies its referent; it cannot be applied without uneasiness to someone one loves; saying "he" about someone, I always envision a kind of murder by language, whose entire scene, sometimes sumptuous, even ceremonial, is *gossip*.

And sometimes, the mockery of all this, "he" gives way to "I" under the simple effect of a syntactic confusion: for in an extended sentence, "he" can refer without warning to many other referents than me.

Here is a series of outdated propositions (if they were not contradictory): *I would be nothing if I didn't write. Yet I am elsewhere than where I am when I write. I am worth more than what I write.*

Un mauvais sujet politique ~ A political misfit

Aesthetics being the art of seeing the forms detach themselves from causes and goals and constitute an adequate system of values, what could be more contrary to politics? Now he could not rid himself of the aesthetic reflex, he could not help *seeing* in some political behavior he approved of, the form (the formal consistency) which it assumed and which he found, as it turned out, hideous or ridiculous. Thus, especially intolerant of blackmail (for what underlying reason?), it was above all blackmail that he saw in the politics of states. By an even more displaced aesthetic sentiment, the taking of hostages always multiplying in the same form, he came to the point of being disgusted by the mechanical character of these operations: they fell into the discredit of all repetition: *another one!*

what a bore! It was like the refrain of a good song, like the facial tic of a handsome man. Hence, because of a perverse disposition to *see* forms, languages, and repetitions, he gradually became a *political misfit.*

Le surdétermination ~ Overdetermination

Ahmad Al Tifashi (1184–1253), author of *Hearts' Delights,* describes a male prostitute's kiss as follows: he thrusts his tongue into your mouth and turns it obstinately. We may take this for the demonstration of *overdetermined* behavior; for from this erotic practice apparently anything but in conformity with his professional status, Al Tifashi's prostitute derives a triple advantage: he shows his erotic competence, safeguards the image of his virility, and yet compromises his own body very little, whose interior he denies you by this very assault. Where is the principal theme? It is a subject, not complicated (as current opinion says with irritation), but *composed* (as Fourier would have said).

La surdi té à son propre langage ~ Deaf to one's own language

What he listened to, what he could not keep from listening to, wherever he was, was the deafness of others to their own language: he heard them not hearing each other. But as for himself? Did he never hear his own deafness? He struggled to hear himself, but produced in this effort no more than another aural scene, another fiction. Hence to entrust himself to writing: is not writing that language which has renounced producing *the last word,* which lives and breathes by yielding itself up to others so that they can hear you?

La symbolique d'État ~ Symbolics of State

I am writing this on Saturday, April 6, 1974, a day of national mourning in memory of Pompidou. All day long, on the radio, "good music" (to my ears): Bach, Mozart, Brahms, Schubert.

L'espace du séminaire est phalanstérien, c'est-
à-dire, en un sens, romanesque. C'est seulement
l'espace de circulation des désirs subtils, des désirs
mobiles; c'est, dans l'artifice d'une socialité
dont la consistance est miraculeusement exténuée,
selon un mot de Nietzsche : "l'enchevêtrement des
rapports amoureux"

The space of the seminar is phalansteric, i.e., in a
sense, fictive, novelistic. It is only the space of the
circulation of subtle desires, mobile desires; it is,
within the artifice of a sociality whose consistency is
miraculously extenuated, according to a phrase of
Nietzsche's: "the tangle of amorous relations"

"Good music," then, is funereal music: an official metonymy unites death, spirituality, and the music of a certain class (on strike days, the radio plays only "bad music"). My neighbor, who ordinarily listens to pop music, doesn't turn on her radio today. Thus we are both excluded from the symbolics of State: she because she does not endure the signifier ("good music"), I because I do not endure the signified (Pompidou's death). Doesn't this double amputation make the music, thus manipulated, into an oppressive discourse?

Le texte symptomal ~ The text as symptom

How can I manage to keep each of these fragments from never being anything but a *symptom?* —Easy: let yourself go, *regress.*

Système / systématique ~ System / systematics

Is it not the characteristic of reality to be *unmasterable?* And is it not the characteristic of any system to *master* it? What then, confronting reality, can one do who rejects mastery? Get rid of the system as apparatus, accept *systematics* as writing (as Fourier did).

Tactique / stratégie ~ Tactics / strategy

The movement of his work is tactical: a matter of displacing himself, of obstructing, as with bars, but not of conquering. Examples: the notion of intertext? It has actually no positivity; it serves to combat the law of context; *acknowledgment* is made at a certain moment as a value, but not out of exaltation of objectivity, instead to oppose the expressivity of bourgeois art; the work's ambiguity has nothing to do with the New Criticism and does not interest him in itself; it is only a little machine for making war against philological law, the academic tyranny of correct meaning. This work would therefore be defined as: *a tactics without strategy.*

He has a certain foible of providing "introductions," "sketches," "elements," postponing the "real" book till later. This foible has a rhetorical name: *prolepsis* (well discussed by Genette).

Here are some of these projected books: a History of Writing, a History of Rhetoric, a History of Etymology, a new Stylistics, an Aesthetics of textual pleasure, a new linguistic science, a Linguistics of Value, an inventory of the languages of love, a fiction based on the notion of an urban Robinson Crusoe, a summa on the *petite bourgeoisie,* a book on France entitled—in the manner of Michelet—*Our France,* etc.

These projects, generally heralding a summative, excessive book, parodic of the great monument of knowledge, can only be simple acts of discourse (prolepses indeed); they belong to the category of the dilatory. But the dilatory, denial of reality (of the realizable), is no less alive for all that: these projects live, they are never abandoned; suspended, they can return to life at any moment; or at least, like the persistent trace of an obsession, they fulfill themselves, partially, indirectly, *as gestures,* through themes, fragments, articles: the History of Writing (postulated in 1953) engenders twenty years later the idea of a seminar on a history of French discourse; the Linguistics of Value, however remotely, orients this very book. *The mountain gives birth to a mouse?* This disdainful proverb must be reversed in a positive sense: the mountain is not any too much to make a mouse.

Fourier never describes his books as anything but the heralds of the perfect Book, which he will publish later (perfectly clear, perfectly persuasive, perfectly complex). The Annunciation of the Book (the *Prospectus*) is one of those dilatory maneuvers which control our internal utopia. I imagine, I fantasize, I embellish, and I polish the great book of which I am incapable: it is a book of learning and of writing, at once a perfect system and the mockery of all systems, a summa of intelligence and of pleasure, a vengeful and tender book, corrosive and pacific, etc. (here, a foam of adjectives,

an explosion of the image-repertoire); in short, it has all the quali-
ties of a hero in a novel: it is the one coming (the *adventure*), and I
herald this book that makes me my own John the Baptist, I proph-
esy, I announce . . .

If he often foresees books to write (which he does not write),
it is because he postpones until later what bores him. Or rather, he
wants to write *right away* what it pleases him to write, and not
something else. In Michelet, what makes him want to rewrite are
those carnal themes, the coffee, the blood, the sisal, the wheat,
etc.; thus one will construct a thematic criticism for oneself, but in
order not to risk it theoretically against another school—historical,
biographical, etc.—for the fantasy is too egoistic to be polemical,
one declares that one is concerned with no more than a *pre-
criticism,* and that the "real" criticism (which is that of other people) will come later.

Being incessantly short of time (or you imagine yourself to
be), caught up in deadlines and delays, you persist in supposing
that you are going to get out of it by putting what you have to do in
order. You make programs, draw up plans, calendars, new deadlines. On your desk and in your files, how many lists of articles,
books, seminars, courses to teach, telephone calls to make. As a
matter of fact, you never consult these little slips of paper, given
the fact that an anguished conscience has provided you with an ex-
cellent memory of all your obligations. But it is irrepressible: you
extend the time you lack by the very registration of that lack. Let us
call this *program compulsion* (whose hypomaniacal character one
readily divines); states and collectivities, apparently, are not exempt from it: how much time wasted in *drawing up programs?* And
since I anticipate writing an article on it, the very notion of program itself becomes a part of my program compulsion.

Now let us reverse all this: these dilatory maneuvers, these
endlessly receding projects may be writing itself. First of all, the
work is never anything but the meta-book (the temporary commentary) of a work to come which, *not being written,* becomes this

work itself: Proust, Fourier never wrote anything but such a "Prospectus." Afterward, the work is never monumental: it is a *proposition* which each will come to saturate as he likes, as he can: I bestow upon you a certain semantic substance to run through, like a ferret. Finally, the work is a (theatrical) *rehearsal,* and this rehearsal, as in one of Rivette's films, is verbose, infinite, interlaced with commentaries, excursuses, shot through with other matters. In a word, the work is a tangle; its being is the *degree,* the step: a staircase that never stops.

Tel Quel ~ *Tel Quel*

His friends on *Tel Quel:* their originality, their *truth* (aside from their intellectual energy, their genius for writing) insist that they must agree to speak a common, general, incorporeal language, i.e., political language, *although each of them speaks it with his own body.* —Then why don't you do the same thing? —Precisely, no doubt, because I do not have the same body that they do; my body cannot accommodate itself to *generality,* to the power of generality which is in language. —Isn't that an individualistic view? Wouldn't one expect to hear it from a Christian—a notorious anti-Hegelian—such as Kierkegaard?

The body is the irreducible difference, and at the same time it is the principle of all structuration (since structuration is what is Unique in structure). If I managed to talk politics *with my own body,* I should make out of the most banal of (discursive) structures a structuration; with repetition, I should produce Text. The problem is to know if the political apparatus would recognize for very long this way of escaping the militant banality by thrusting into it— alive, pulsing, pleasure-seeking—my own unique body.

Le temps qu'il fait ~ What the weather is doing

This morning the woman in the bakery said: *It's still lovely, but the heat's lasting too long!* (people around here always feel that it's too lovely, too hot). I add: *And the light is so beautiful!* But the

175

woman does not answer, and once again I notice that short-circuit in language of which the most trivial conversations are the sure occasion; I realize that *seeing the light* relates to a class sensibility; or rather, since there are "picturesque" lights which are certainly enjoyed by the woman in the bakery, what is socially marked is the "vague" view, the view without contours, without object, *without figuration,* the view of a transparency, the view of a non-view (that unfigurative value which occurs in good painting and never in bad). In short, nothing more cultural than the atmosphere, nothing more ideological than what the weather is doing.

Terre promise ~ Promised land

He regretted not being able to embrace all avant-gardes at once, he regretted being limited, too conventional, etc.; and his regret could be illuminated by no sure analysis: just what was it he was resisting? What was he rejecting (or even more superficially: what was he *sulking over*) in one place or another? A style? An arrogance? A violence? An imbecility?

Ma tête s'embrouille ~ My head is confused

On a certain kind of work, on a certain kind of subject (usually the ones dissertations are made of), on a certain day of life itself, he would like to be able to post as a motto this old-wives' remark: *My head is confused* (let us imagine a language in which the set of grammatical categories would sometimes force the subject to speak in the aspect of an old woman).

And yet: *at the level of his body,* his head never gets confused. It is a curse: no value, lost, secondary state: always consciousness: drugs excluded, yet he dreams of them: dreams of being able to intoxicate himself (instead of getting sick right away); anticipating from a surgical operation for at least once in his life an *absence,* which was denied him for lack of a general anesthesia; recovering every morning, upon waking, a head swimming a little, but whose interior remains fixed (sometimes, falling to sleep with something worrying me, upon first waking it has disappeared; a white minute, miraculously stripped of meaning; but the worry rushes upon me, like a bird of prey, and I find myself altogether back where I was, *just as I was the day before*).

Sometimes he feels like letting all this language rest—this language which is in his head, in his work, in other people, as if language itself were an exhausted limb of the human body; it seems to him that if he could take a rest from language, he could rest altogether, dismissing all crises, echoes, exaltations, injuries, reasonings, etc. He sees language in the figure of an exhausted old woman (something like an antique cleaning woman with worn hands) who sighs for a certain *retirement* . . .

Le théâtre ~ Theater

At the crossroads of the entire *oeuvre,* perhaps the Theater: there is not a single one of his texts, in fact, which fails to deal with a certain theater, and spectacle is the universal category in whose aspect the world is seen. The theater relates to all the apparently special themes which pass and return in what he writes: connotation, hysteria, fiction, the image-repertoire, the scene, grace, the Orient, violence, ideology (which Bacon once called a "phantom of theatre"). What has attracted him is less the sign than the signal, the poster: the science he desired was not a semiology but a *signaletics.*

Not believing in the separation of affect and sign, of the emotion and its theater, he could not *express* an admiration, an indignation, a love, for fear of signifying it badly. Hence, the more moved he was, the more lusterless. His "serenity" was merely the constraint of an actor who dares not come on stage lest he perform too badly.

Incapable of making himself convincing to himself, yet it is the very conviction of others which in his eyes makes them into creatures of theater and fascinates him. He asks the actor to show him a convinced body, rather than a true passion. Here perhaps is the best theater he has ever seen: in the Belgian dining car, certain employees (customs officer, policemen) were sitting at a corner table; they ate their meal with so much appetite, comfort, and care (choosing the spices, the pieces, the appropriate tableware, preferring at a knowing glance the steak to the insipid chicken), with manners so perfectly applied to the food (carefully scraping off their fish the suspect cream sauce, tapping their yogurt in order to remove the seal, scratching their cheese instead of peeling it, using their fruit knife as if it were a scalpel), that the whole Cook service was subverted: they were eating the same things as we were, but it was not the same menu. Everything had changed, from one end of the car to the other, by the single effect of a *conviction* (relation of the body not to passion or to the soul but to pleasure, to bliss).

Le thème ~ The theme

Thematic criticism has come under a certain suspicion in recent years. Yet we must not abandon this critical notion too readily. The theme is a useful notion to designate that site of discourse where the body advances *under its own responsibility,* and thereby thwarts the sign: the "gnarled," for instance, is neither signifier nor signified, or both at once: it pins down here and at the same time refers farther away. In order to make the theme into a structural concept, a certain etymological delirium is necessary: as the structural units are in one case or another "morphemes," "phonemes," "monemes," "gustemes," "vestemes," "erotemes," "biographemes," etc. Let us imagine, according to the same formation, that the "theme" is the structural unit of the thesis (ideal discourse): what is posited, outlined, advanced by the utterance, and remains as *the availability of the meaning* (before being, occasionally, its fossil).

Conversion de la valeur en théorie
~ Conversion of value into theory

Conversion of Value into Theory (distractedly, I read on my file card: "convulsion," which is fine too): one might say, parodying Chomsky, that all Value is *rewritten* (→) as Theory. This conversion—this convulsion—is an energy (an *energon*): discourse is produced by this translation, this imaginary displacement, this creation of an alibi. Having originated in value (which does not mean that it is any the less warranted for that), theory becomes an intellectual object, and this object is caught up into a larger circulation (it encounters a different *image-system* of the reader).

La maxime ~ The maxim

An aphoristic tone hangs about this book (*we, one, always*). Now the maxim is compromised in an essentialist notion of human nature, it is linked to classical ideology: it is the most arrogant (often the stupidest) of the forms of language. Why then not reject it? The reason is, as always, emotive: I write maxims (or I sketch their movement) *in order to reassure myself:* when some disturbance arises, I attenuate it by confiding myself to a fixity which exceeds my powers: *"Actually, it's always like that":* and the maxim is born. The maxim is a sort of *sentence-name,* and to name is to pacify. Moreover, this too is a maxim: it attenuates my fear of seeking extravagance by writing maxims.

(Telephone call from X: he tells me about his vacation, but never asks a single question about mine, as if I had not stirred for the last two months. I do not regard this as indifference; rather the demonstration of a defense: *where I wasn't present, the world has remained motionless:* great security. It is in this fashion that the immobility of the maxim reassures perturbed organizations.)

Le monstre de la totalité ~ The monster of totality

"Let us imagine (if we can) a woman covered with an endless

garment, itself woven of everything said in the fashion magazine . . ." (*Système de la Mode*). This imagination, apparently methodical since it merely sets up an operative notion of semantic analysis ("the endless text"), actually (secretly) aims at denouncing the monster of Totality (Totality as monster). Totality at one and the same time inspires laughter and fear: like violence, is it not always *grotesque* (and then recuperable only in an aesthetics of Carnival)?

Different discourse: this August 6, the countryside, the morning of a splendid day: sun, warmth, flowers, silence, calm, radiance. Nothing stirs, neither desire nor aggression; only the task is there, the work before me, like a kind of universal being: everything is full. Then that would be Nature? An absence . . . of the rest? Totality?

August 6, 1973–September 3, 1974

To write the body.
Neither the skin, nor the muscles, nor the bones,
nor the nerves, but the rest: an awkward, fibrous,
shaggy, raveled thing, a clown's coat

Pl. IX

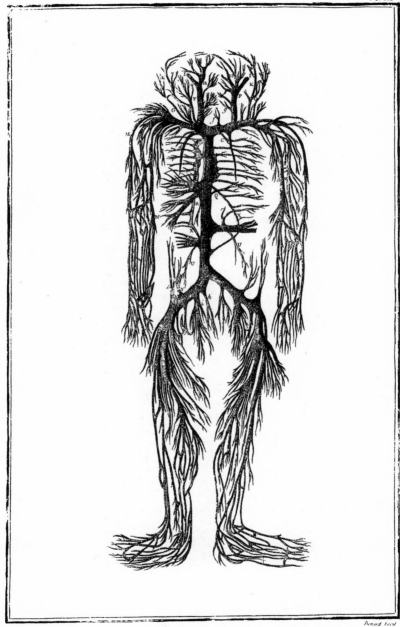

Anatomie

Biography

November 12, 1915	Born in Cherbourg, son of Louis Barthes, naval officer, and Henriette Binger.
October 26, 1916	Death of Louis Barthes, in a naval battle on the North Sea.
1916–24	Childhood in Bayonne. Elementary-school classes in the lycée of this city.
1924	Move to Paris, rue Mazarine and rue Jacques-Callot. Henceforth, all school vacations spent with the Barthes grandparents, in Bayonne.
1924–30	At Lycée Montaigne, from the eighth form to the fourth.
1930–4	At Lycée Louis-le-Grand, from the third form to Philosophy. Baccalaureates: 1933 and 1934.
May 10, 1934	Hemophthisis. Lesion in the left lung.
1934–5	Treatment in the Pyrénées, at Bedous, in the Aspe valley.
1935–9	Sorbonne: license in classical letters. Foundation of the Groupe de Théâtre Antique.
1937	Exempted from military service. —Reader during the summer at Debreczen (Hungary).
1938	Trip to Greece with the Groupe de Théâtre Antique.
1939–40	Professor of fourth and third forms (rectoral delegate) at the new lycée of Biarritz.
1940–1	Rectoral delegate (tutor and professor) at the Lycées Voltaire and Carnot, in Paris. —Diplôme d'études supérieures (on Greek tragedy).

October 1941	Relapse of pulmonary tuberculosis.
1942	First stay in the Sanatorium des Étudiants, at Saint-Hilaire-du-Touvet, in the Isère.
1943	Convalescence at the Post-Cure in the rue Quatrefages, in Paris. —Final license (grammar and philology).
July 1943	Relapse in the right lung.
1943–5	Second stay in the Sanatorium des Étudiants. Silence treatment, slope treatment, etc. In the sanatorium, several months of pre-medical study with the intention of pursuing psychiatric medicine. During treatment, relapse.
1945–6	Subsequent treatment at Leysin, at the Clinique Alexandre, part of the Sanatorium Universitaire Suisse.
October 1945	Right extra-pleural pneumothorax.
1946–7	Convalescence in Paris.
1948–9	Assistant librarian, then professor at the Institut français of Bucharest, and reader in the university of this city.
1949–50	Reader at the University of Alexandria (Egypt).
1950–2	At the Direction générale des Relations culturelles, instruction branch.
1952–4	Officer of Instruction at the Centre National de Recherche Scientifique (lexicology).
1954–5	Literary adviser to Éditions de l'Arche.
1955–9	Research attaché at the C.N.R.S. (sociology).
1960–2	Chairman of the VI section of the École pratique des Hautes Études (social and economic sciences).
1962	Director of studies at the École pratique des Hautes Études ("Sociology of signs, symbols, and representations").

(A life: studies, diseases, appointments. And the rest? Encounters, friendships, loves, travels, readings, pleasures, fears, beliefs, satisfactions, indignations, distresses: in a word: repercussions? —In the text—but not in the work.)

Illustrations

186

Doodling . . .

or the signifier without the signified

Et après ?

— Quoi écrire, maintenant ? Pourrez-
vous encore écrire quelque chose ?
— On écrit avec son désir, et je
n'en finis pas de désirer.

And afterward?
–What to write now? Can you still write anything?
–One writes with one's desire, and I am not through
desiring.